STEVEN SPIELBERG

NURS
OFFIC

Steven Spielberg

A Life in Films

MOLLY HASKELL

Yale
UNIVERSITY
PRESS
New Haven and London

Frontispiece: Spielberg and Henry Thomas discuss a scene in *E.T. the Extraterrestrial.* Universal Pictures/Photofest.

Yale University Press books may be purchased in quantity for educational, business, or promotional use. For information, please e-mail sales.press@yale.edu (U.S. office) or sales@yaleup.co.uk (U.K. office).

Set in Janson Oldstyle type by Tseng Information Systems, Inc.
Printed in the United States of America.

Library of Congress Control Number: 2016938134
ISBN 978-0-300-18693-2 (hardcover : alk. paper)

A catalogue record for this book is available from the British Library.

This paper meets the requirements of ANSI/NISO Z39.48-1992 (Permanence of Paper).

10 9 8 7 6 5 4 3 2 1

CONTENTS

PREFACE

IN EARLY 1993, Steven Spielberg is in Kraków filming *Schindler's List.* By day, he shoots a scene in a work camp: children are being herded onto trucks for deportation, singing as if on a jolly field trip. A few run away to crouch in cellars and boxes, and when there are no more hiding places, one jumps into a latrine. By night, he is talking via satellite with the crew at Industrial Light and Magic in northern California, discussing the final editing of *Jurassic Park,* listening to John Williams's score, maybe fiddling with the elbow of a velociraptor. The juxtaposition—as if dread and anxiety could thus be halved, one film allaying the stress of the other—seems almost inhuman as well as superhuman.

In December 2016, Spielberg turned seventy. In his eighth decade on earth, he is still making movies as fast we can see them. What keeps him going? The answer, or rather the mystery, begins with the outsize fears of a little boy who began biting his nails while still in knee-pants. A little boy who was spooked by everything, by the static on the radio, by Disney films, by the tree outside his New Jersey window that turned sinister in a storm, its branches weaving and waving like some otherworldly monster.

What makes him unusual is not just the size of the fears but his manner of hanging onto them. Rather than bury those shaming moments of childhood vulnerability, as most of us do, he nourished their memory, translated them into bold cinematic images, and projected them onto a terrified audience as he had once relieved his own anxiety by terrorizing his younger sisters. So powerful was the urge—and so successful an exorcism—that as a director he would aim for nothing less than whole theaters full of spectators biting their nails, or blissed out with shock and awe at close encounters with the paranormal.

In the weeks leading up to the 2014 Academy Awards, one of the factoids that newscasters dished out to whet viewer appetites was a statistic on who Oscar winners thanked most. The top two names, according to NBC's Lester Holt, were Steven Spielberg and God, with the latter receiving only nineteen mentions to the former's forty-two. What did this mean? That he has touched more lives and boosted more careers than the Almighty, let alone L. B. Mayer, David Selznick, Irving Thalberg, Lew Wasserman, and assorted agents, parents, and spouses? Or perhaps that the popular populist has simply become a lodestar to would-be filmmakers, like the celestial light in *Close Encounters of the Third Kind*, or the extraterrestrial pal E.T. Or even that his philanthropic work, like the establishment of the Shoah Foundation, with its archived testimonies from Holocaust survivors, has granted him a transcendent place among mankind's beneficiaries.

The output is staggering; his fingerprints are everywhere, as producer as well as director, in video games and television as well as feature films. In his forty-two years of making movies—

fifty-two if you count his childhood efforts—the wunderkind has given more pleasure to more people than any other filmmaker in history. If he hasn't touched every heart and mind with every picture, it's a guarantee that he has touched even the harshest critic with one, or two, or three. For some, the early movies centering on childhood—*Close Encounters* and *E.T.*—have never been bettered. For others *Jaws*, *Raiders of the Lost Ark*, and *Jurassic Park* are the greatest adventure movies ever made, and even their weaker spin-offs and sequels have a way of earning, with time, the revisionist honor of "underappreciated gems." For still others, like myself, the later films with their dark edges—*Empire of the Sun*, *Schindler's List*, *A.I.*, *Minority Report*, and the melancholy-tinged *Catch Me If You Can*—give a greater and very different kind of pleasure.

Other action movies and franchises may equal or outperform his at the box office, but no filmmaker has combined profits and prestige the way he has, with multiple Oscar nominations and wins, while at the same time having directed—with figures adjusted for inflation—two of the top ten grossing films of all time, *E.T. the Extra-Terrestrial* and *Jaws*. The box office flops are few, and generally the artistic failures and underperformers go on to recoup their investment in global release or on DVD. Financial success is also part of the story, offputting to many and a critical liability, but something that has enabled him to follow his conscience into less crowd-pleasing movies and accomplish a great deal as a philanthropist.

When Yale University Press came to me with the idea of writing a short biography of Spielberg for its Jewish Lives series, I hesitated, for obvious and less obvious reasons. I didn't worry about not being Jewish—let others do that. I believe strongly that there should be no bars of race, ethnicity, or gender to writing, and I think it's particularly important in the case of Spielberg, for one of his greatest traits has always been a kind of natural ecumenism, a generosity of spirit. He grew up in mostly gentile suburbs in New Jersey and Arizona and belatedly found his own path to Judaism, coming to terms with the faith he'd denied and the insults he'd suffered, but remarkably free of rancor or a retributive agenda.

More to the point, I had never been an ardent fan. We both had our blind spots. The problem was, Spielberg's blind spots were my *see* spots, and vice versa. He readily acknowledged that he had no feeling for European films. He always wanted his films to "arrive" someplace. But brooding ambiguities, unresolved longings, things left unsaid, and the erotic transactions of men and women are the very things that drew me to movies in the first place. His great subjects—children, adolescents—and genres—science fiction, fantasy, horror, action-adventure—were stay-away zones for me. Even his forays into history were inspirational rather than ironic or fatalistic, the work of a man who favored moral clarity, was uncomfortable with "shades of gray."

Nor was I—nor had I ever been—the adolescent boy whose fears and anxieties were the gnawing, liberating center of his films, who would respond passionately to his oeuvre, resisting, with him, the ordeal of growing up and moving on. I had been born a different gender and six significant years earlier, a war baby as opposed to the boomers of which he (born in 1946) was an entry-level member. Mine was an in-between sensibility: although I would rebel and make a break for broader pastures, adults were still figures of fascination and respect.

I worried more about my biases, my inherent lack of sympathy as a woman, as a person, for the genres in which Spielberg had enjoyed his greatest successes. I was never susceptible to the wonderments of fantasy or the supernatural, whose delights, like the cacophonous thrills of car crashes and train wrecks, belonged to a boy's world. Yes, fangirls, many of you respond to vampires and werewolves and dystopic science fiction, as *Twilight* and *The Hunger Games* have demonstrated, and conversely, many men are indifferent to its charms. Still, the fears that Spielberg played with so brilliantly struck me primarily as men's fears—of women, of maturity, of sex.

Some of us were hard on his early films. (So hard that, looking back, I was shocked at the intemperate tone of our reviews.) I was a True Believer, in something more magical than UFOs, a crusader in what would later be called the great age of "cinephilia," seeing and reevaluating the glories of the past, rushing to see and talk about exciting new auteurist films from Europe and America.

This sense of peril and a certain foreboding is what we felt when suddenly (somewhere around 1973) the conversation was all about money: "saturation" marketing, must-see summer films, the advent of the blockbuster, and then the high drama of the weekend opening and the box office intake.

Trying to come to terms with this man who has had such an outsize influence on our lives seemed like a worthy challenge. In grappling with Spielberg I would be confronting my own resistance. Moreover, there were many Spielberg films that I did love and looked forward to seeing again . . . and came to admire even more the second or third time around. And the man has worn extraordinarily well. Naysayers have been turned into yea-sayers as critics have come to appreciate the sheer versatility of his moviemaking skills. He's a deft deployer of the latest in CGI techniques and video, but is a deep-in-his-bones lover of the look and texture of classic film. If he and George Lucas were responsible for catapulting science fiction into the big-budget stratosphere, Spielberg's movies displayed a feeling, lacking in the efforts of many of his followers, for actual human beings. His instincts—the way his genre and period films resonate with present-day anxieties—have proved so unerring as to be uncanny. There is nothing ironic or "cutting-edge" about him, and that has proved refreshing: his history epics are told in straightforward fashion and celebrate an old-fashioned sense of virtue, transmitting the best of a tradition we've come to appreciate in its absence.

Oddly enough, there were certain common points between Spielberg and me. We were both squares come to the big city, products of fifties suburban America, repressed in different ways, looking for something. If we weren't exactly apolitical, neither of us was inflamed by radical activities or attitudes. Spielberg's middle America was not the circle of hell favored by most filmmakers, nor was he biased against "the establishment," so when his films did become more concerned with human carelessness and criminality, the darkness was earned.

Would Spielberg speak to me? I made inquiries. No, his assistant emailed me, he had a policy of not granting interviews to biographers. It was true he hadn't given an interview to Joseph McBride, who seems to have talked to everybody else and to whose superb biography I am deeply indebted. Still, I felt stung, a little red-faced, like a girl angling for a date and being rejected.

There also may have been a bit of a grudge: While watching clips of Spielberg on YouTube, I came upon one from 1978 where he is speaking with directorial aspirants in a master class at the American Film Institute. He looks as young as or younger than his audience members but has chalked up two monster successes, of which they seem quite suspicious. Is he in it for the money? What will he do now? He has said earlier that he is not a director who imposes his style like Orson Welles, but rather a craftsman like Victor Fleming, the studio go-to man for big pictures like *The Wizard of Oz* and *Gone with the Wind.* Then, smiling from under his baseball cap, he says, "You just have to have confidence. You can't worry if critics like Andrew Sarris and Molly Haskell don't like your movies."

I winced. But I also fell a little in love with him at that moment, with his charm and quick-wittedness, his playful faux-modesty, and—most erotic to a movie lover—his obvious knowledge of and passion for films. His spurning of me personally came to seem a relief. I'd have been compromised. Either through natural sympathy or good manners, I'd have felt inhibited, seduced into his point of view, unable to maintain a critical distance. The sense of personal liking was strong, and buoyed me while slogging through massive amounts of material and trying to figure out how to write a "short" biography of a man still dauntingly alive and around whose career the (critical) dust was far from settled. I wanted to do justice to the life, and the fascinating issue of his Jewishness—denied, then embraced. But because of who he was ("Everything about me is in my films") and who I was, I needed to tell it through the movies. I take it as by now axiomatic that film criticism is personal, never "objective" or unbiased, and biography can evaluate as well as report. To tell the story of Spielberg through his films is to take into account one's own engagements, and the way time and context—politics, world events, other films—alter everything. We and the films age and change. Considerations of box office and marketing and hyperbole recede in time, the glories of art endure.

STEVEN SPIELBERG

1

Beginnings and the Lost Ark

It's the late sixties and early seventies, the Age of Aquarius. America is at war with the Communists in Southeast Asia and at war with itself at home. Political agitators turn violent, plays and movies bristle with drill sergeant language, counterculture rebels are slashing icons and reinventing genres. But Hollywood, our national Colosseum, is missing out on the action, being mired in the mindset and operational mode of the studio system of the fifties. The tremors of change are elsewhere: one hundred miles up the Pacific coast at Nicholas Beach, where a motley group of auteur wannabes, film school nerds, and showbiz bohemians hang out and smoke dope and conspire to take over the industry. Their crash pad is a ramshackle house rented by actresses Jennifer Salt and Margot Kidder. Julia and Michael Phillips, producers of the Oscar-winning *The Sting* (1973), will buy a neighboring house, and host week-long drug-fueled soirees, described in Julia's own gonzo-ish memoir, *You'll Never Eat Lunch in This Town Again.*[1]

The guest list will feature such drop-by celebrities as Robert Redford and Liza Minnelli and, from up the beach, literary lights Joan Didion and John Gregory Dunne, but most of the gang, high on drugs and European movies, are unknown or barely known filmmakers like Francis Ford Coppola and Marty Scorsese, Paul Schrader and John Milius and Brian De Palma, George and Marcia Lucas, all film school graduates. Julia casts her beady eye on "a rogues' gallery of nerds . . . slim pickin's from a woman's point of view," adding, "I wouldn't have gone out with any of them in high school." But the guys—thanks no doubt to the influence of Julia, who is getting through pregnancy with a pharmacopeia of Quaaludes, coke, uppers, and downers—are at least learning to act cool and get laid.

Standing apart, the misfit in the picture, is a guy in a baseball cap, clean-shaven, shirt and jacket, maybe even a tie, maybe even a virgin, and definitely "clean," determined to keep his brain booze- and drug-free. The guy is Steven Spielberg, fresh from his day job at Universal Studios, where he has been directing television episodes of *Marcus Welby*, *Columbo*, *Night Gallery*, keeping his nose to the grindstone while his contemporaries are using theirs as delivery systems. The early starter who couldn't do sports or campfires and got his Boy Scout badge by making a movie is probably more proficient with a camera, knows more intimately the excitement of putting shots together, than a whole classroom of film school graduates. He's not crazy about working in television, but he didn't have the grades to get into film school at USC, so he's learning to edit, developing strategies for dealing with divas, acquiring discipline—not a top priority for this renegade crowd.

They are the cool guys and visionaries, with grand plans for remaking the studio system. Coppola (born 1939), no slouch, has already made five films and won three Academy Awards by

1972, the year of *The Godfather*, and started Zoetrope, his own studio, in 1969. George Lucas (1944) will open a studio too; his age and career closely parallel Spielberg's, and his *THX-1138*, which started as a student film in 1969, blew Spielberg's mind. Paul Schrader (1946), breaking away with a vengeance from his Calvinist upbringing, writes *The Yakuza* in 1974 and *Taxi Driver* in 1976. Martin Scorsese (1942), NYU Film School graduate, will direct *Mean Streets* in 1973. Brian De Palma (1940) begins modestly with the offbeat *Greetings* and *Hi, Mom* and goes on to *Carrie* in 1976. John Milius (1944), the tough guy of the bunch, will bring a modern intensity to action pictures.

Anxious studio czars, still stuck in a postwar era of censorship and high-gloss stars, are shaken by movies like *Easy Rider*, *Bonnie and Clyde*, *The Graduate*. They continue to make old-fashioned family pictures and win Oscars for movies like *In the Heat of the Night* and *Oliver!*, but movies are becoming less Waspy glamorous, more ethnic. Without confronting the war or the Kennedy assassination directly, the new films are seeded by that era's themes of guilt, pessimism, futility. The aesthetic is grittier, the stories often bleak or open-ended, a radical departure from the old narrative playbooks. The guys (yes, they were all guys) responsible for those game-changing films are in love with the *Nouvelle Vague*, Fellini and Antonioni. Movies of the sixties like *Faces*, *Easy Rider*, and *Dr. Strangelove*, and Robert Altman's 1970 *M*A*S*H*, have made the world safe for a new kind of studio-financed independent film.

The new guys' collective euphoria will prove to be a media moment rather than a changing of the guard, a rejuvenation rather than a revolution. Hollywood's taste for personal directors will fade after a couple of *folies des grandeurs* like *Apocalypse Now* and Michael Cimino's *Heaven's Gate*. Two squares from suburbia would bring Hollywood back to its comfort zone.

Of course, neat divisions between hip and square, one era and another, are journalistic conveniences that conceal as much as they reveal, no less an oversimplification than the notion of a strict separation between Hollywood and independent cinema. The Monkees were as much a part of the sixties as Bob Dylan.

Nevertheless, the two new Hollywoods are present on that beach, though they don't quite know it at the time. What they all have in common along with directorial ambition is that movies are their language, their grammar, their poetry. Their heads are filled with camera movements rather than words, they're high on the movies they will make, and their excitement is echoed by a seriousness about American films among a new breed of critics writing in the underground and alternate weeklies, gradually migrating to the mainstream press.

Unlike the others, Steven started out not as a movie buff but a child of television. He didn't read film books or seek out revivals. His apprenticeship was strictly hands-on with a movie camera, and then, when he did begin gorging on Hollywood cinema, it was the craftsmen and the epic filmmakers to whom he was drawn. While De Palma and Scorsese, at least for the moment, are thinking small (homages to Fellini and Hitchcock), Steven imagines widescreen epics, like David Lean's *Lawrence of Arabia*, or (the picture that enthralled him as a child) Cecil B. DeMille's *The Greatest Show on Earth*. His mentor-idols are not the auteurs but journeymen like Victor Fleming and borderline auteur Michael Curtiz.

While the others were cultivating their outsider status as artist-moviemakers with personal visions, Spielberg, with his complex, mostly subterranean relationship with his Jewishness, wanted only to fit in. His father was a workaholic in whose absence he had grown up in a house of free-range females: an artistically inclined permissive mother and three high-spirited younger sisters. Even the dog, he once complained, was female.

Another common thread is the male-oriented cinema to which both the edgy and the more conventional upstarts will gravitate. These twenty- and thirty-somethings have grown up in the flight path of two of the greatest upheavals in history: feminism and the technological revolution. In mere seconds of evolutionary time, women had gone from winning the vote to running for office, and computers had evolved from servants to masters. Whether expressed in science-fiction fantasies or toga parties, cartoon heroes or supermacho action movies, male anxiety lurks ever closer to the surface. Unlike the more romantic or erotically driven cinema of pathbreaking elders like Woody Allen, Paul Mazursky, John Cassavetes, Robert Altman, Arthur Penn, lovers and likers of women, these newcomers were all, in different ways, in flight from women.

In the film industry, the sense of threat—from women on the one hand, and from machines and Artificial Intelligence on the other—will form a leitmotif that runs like a threnody through all these filmmakers' work. The male-female equilibrium, always breathtakingly precarious in, say, screwball comedy and film noir, had already begun to topple in the fifties.

Spielberg would not be alone in rarely if ever featuring an interesting complex woman at the fore or even an adult sexual relationship. And by sexual I don't mean specific portrayal of sex, but a feeling for the chemistry of attraction that is a sort of baseline language not just in European films, but even, perhaps especially, in old Hollywood films. With the crumbling of taboos, love and marriage were no longer forever; diversity of race and sexual orientation meant a dethroning of the Wasp couple as the all-purpose embodiment of romantic fantasies.

The Nerd is preparing his Revenge. As an outsider in his teenage years, both Jewish and a non-jock, Spielberg understood doubly the insecurities of the awkward adolescent, and he would tap into the vulnerability of the male in a more direct way than either Judd Apatow or the testosterone-pumped action flicks. He wasn't interested in superheroes, in outsize hulks and transformers, or in suavely invulnerable Bond-like protagonists. And while Apatow's schlubby antiheroes were smoking pot and ogling girls while resisting marriage and fatherhood, Spielberg with less jaded eyes would tap into the spirit of regression by spinning fairy tales out of infancy and youth, infusing them with a holy aura and raising them to new heights of meaning and artistic seriousness.

One of the most appealing aspects of Spielberg is his disarming candor: throughout his long career, he has known—and, what's more, acknowledged—where his strengths and weaknesses lay. He didn't try for sex, or for grown-up romance, because he wasn't good at it. And he wasn't one of the political or lifestyle radicals. From the early age at which he began planning his career, he knew he stood on the commercial side of the split between art and commerce. I am my audience, he would say—and this turned out to be amazingly, astoundingly, continually true, as he and they aged. He could have been anticipating the split between the square and the cool at the Nicholas Beach gatherings when he told the story on himself, in a short film called *Amblin'*, made in 1968 as his "calling card" to the studios. I'll describe this remarkable first effort in more detail later, but suffice to say that between the two main characters, a hippie and a square, the latter is clearly and candidly the Spielberg surrogate.

And the hippie girl? A nod, perhaps, to free spirits like Jennifer and Margot, but might she not also be a sixties rendition of that primal free spirit, Steven's mother, Leah, the anything-goes mom, the fairy godmother, who grants her son his every wish. She was "more coconspirator than parent," he told Lesley Stahl in 2012 on *60 Minutes*.[2] Included in the segment was a separate interview with both of his long-divorced parents—charming and seemingly congenial. "We never said no," Leah Adler confessed. "Anything he wanted, we did. Steve really did run us. He called the shots."

To which Steven added, "My mom didn't parent us as much

as she sort of big-sistered us. She was Peter Pan. She refused to grow up."

It was during the same interview that a revelation occurred. Contrary to the conviction, long held by Steven and expressed in the weak or perfidious father figures of his films, that Arnold was the culprit in the breakup, it turned out that it was Leah who strayed. Leah, the exalted one, the parent on a pedestal, had fallen in love with Arnold's good friend. Arnold conceded in the same interview that he had allowed, even encouraged, this misconception. Why? asked Stahl.

"I don't know," Arnold says, "I think I was just protecting her, because I was in love with her."

"Even though she left you?" Stahl presses.

"Yeah," Arnold admits with a smile, "still do."

Had Steven ever entertained such a suspicion? Had even the vaguest idea of Leah's betrayal existed in the boy's subconscious? If so, he couldn't afford to let it emerge into full awareness. Leah was the caretaker, the heart and soul of the family. He needed for Arnold to be the fall guy, just as he needed to revere his mother as partner, liberator, and saint.

For fifteen years, Steven nourished this myth of villainy and virtue, its powerful hold on his emotions triggering the imaginative configuration of every movie, every male and female character and plot dynamic, contributing to that pre-Oedipal mindset that became both inspiration and limitation. There would be more benign father figures after the revelation, but the impulses of blame and reverence, and the sexual taboos that went with them, would continue to animate the stories. Why would anyone want to "work through" or "resolve" such profitable anxieties?

Steven was born in Cincinnati, where Leah Posner and Arnold Spielberg had grown up, one of the great midwestern boomtowns of the nineteenth century. It was a center for both industry and culture, and a magnet for immigrants, first the English and Dutch in the early part of the century, then Russian and eastern European Jews between 1881 and 1914. It soon became home to one of the largest Jewish populations west of the Alleghenies.

Leah's family, the Posners, had come from Odessa, a city of progressive ideas and cultural ferment, while Arnold's were from a rural and distinctly less worldly area of the Ukraine, Kamenetz-Podolsk. There were ranchers and farmers on his father's side, brewers on his mother's side. The two areas were different in another way: Kamenetz, though not untouched by pogroms, had a less violent history; for long periods, Jews and non-Jews kept to themselves in peaceful coexistence. When Jewish families finally began emigrating, they were driven by a variety of reasons, economic as well as physical. There were restrictions on Jewish labor, and the men were being forced to serve in the czar's army, known for its mistreatment of Jews.

Odessa, however, for all its claims to cosmopolitanism, was far more riven by antisemitic violence. Born there in 1884, Philip Posner witnessed some of the worst anti-Jewish riots in Russian history and finally came to America following the pogroms of 1905—the year of the sailors' mutiny on the battleship *Potemkin*, subject of the great Eisenstein silent film.

Arriving in Cincinnati, he, like many Jews—indeed, like Arnold's own father—began as a pushcart peddler and traveling salesman, eventually working out of his home. Little Steven would spend hours in his attic, playing with Philip's unsold merchandise—a cornucopia which he converted into toys. Arnold's father, who died just before Steven was born, became a jobber, soon acquiring a store and a sales route. He eventually amassed a large sum of money, then lost it all in the Depression.

But the real forces in both families, the dominant figures, were the women. As so often happened, in coming to America the men, unable to get well-paying jobs, fell in social status, while the women took charge. Nor was this just an immigrant pattern: even in Russia, Arnold's grandmother had worked the brewery with her sons while the father studied Torah. And each of Steven's grandmothers—Rebecca Spielberg and Jennie Posner—had been a powerhouse in her own right. In Cincinnati, they not only assumed domestic responsibilities but spread their wings into political and community activities as well. Rebecca (Grandma Becky) was very smart, read avidly, and was active in Jewish organizations and politics while raising three bright children.

Leah's mother, Jennie, the only one of Steven's grandparents to have been born in Cincinnati, was the spark plug whose hunger for education, involvement in political activities, and distinct indifference to domesticity clearly ignited her daughter.

Arnold had grown up in Avondale, a venerable Jewish neighborhood that was itself split between north (German Jews) and south (eastern European Jews). There were non-Jews in Avondale, but by a kind of tacit mutual agreement, both sides kept their distance. The most severe prejudice Arnold remembered experiencing as a child was from German Jews . . . who thought themselves superior "socially, culturally and financially."[3]

It was in Avondale's Adath Israel Synagogue that he and Leah were married. The year was 1945, the end of the war, just before he was demobilized from the U.S. Army. A little over a year later, on December 18, 1946, Steven was born in Avondale's Nonsectarian Jewish Hospital, and it was in Avondale that the Spielbergs, surrounded by extended family, lived for the first two and a half years of Steven's life. Their part of Avondale was mostly middle-aged and older Orthodox Jews, so Steven spent his infancy in a strange sort of cocoon, a beloved child among much older people with few children his own age. His father was attending the University of Cincinnati on the G.I. Bill and burning the midnight oil, while Steven was entrusted to his mother and a circle of grown-ups. His grandmother Jennie, Leah's mother, taught English out of her home to German Jewish immigrants, so at an early age the little boy heard tales of Hitler and the Holocaust, even witnessed tattoos on survivors' arms.

Cincinnati, a locus of the tensions and possibilities of modern Judaism, would take on a progressive cast with the arrival of Rabbi Isaac Mayer Wise. An immigrant from Moravia to New York, and one of the great luminaries of Reform Judaism, the sometimes controversial organizer and unifier had fled Albany after a fistfight with his synagogue's president. He now set about trying to bring cohesion to the many warring forms of religious practice, and under his influence, Cincinnati introduced pioneering institutions like Hebrew Union College, the *American Israelite* newspaper, and the American Jewish Archives. It was also where the eight-day festival of Hanukkah—never a holy feast and barely observed by most of the Jews of the world—would become a contender with Christmas, a bonanza of gift giving and singing, concerts and celebratory activities.

A perfect emblem of the contradictions in Cincinnati's version of twentieth-century Judaism was that thoroughly modern Jennie's husband, Philip, was devoutly and intransigently traditional. Technically, both Posners, though they went to a Conservative synagogue, were Orthodox, but Philip alone wore the Orthodox garb, a long beard, black coat, hat and prayer shawl; and in this pioneering city of reform, he spoke Yiddish and used his Yiddish name, Fievel, refusing to modernize in any way. At the same time, he was a great performer, the singer and storyteller of the family. Leah, who knew whereof she spoke, called him a "frustrated artist." The Spielberg living room would become a stage (*spiel* in German means play!). In addition to Leah at the piano and Fievel singing and dancing, there might also be a solo turn by Great Uncle Boris, Fievel's brother, who had worked briefly as a lion tamer in the circus, a Shakespearean actor in the Yiddish theater, and a vaudevillian complete with straw hat and cane.

To round out the jackpot of showbiz genes to which Steven was heir, Arnold was no mean storyteller himself. But it was Fievel who was like the Chagall image of Shalom Aleichem, the "fiddler" who held everyone spellbound with his music and his portraits of shtetl life in extremis—the joys of community, celebrated in songs and prayer, and the terrors of pogroms.

Despite the progressive atmosphere of midcentury Cincinnati, Avondale itself was an enclave, culturally advanced but, in Leah's mind, claustrophobic. Once again, the Jews had created their own city within a city, with their own schools, rituals, religion, and neighborhoods—the strategy, now instinctive, that had sheltered and protected them through the repeated adversities of history. Now, though, the worst had happened, the worst that so many had known, feared, sensed would happen, and after it the atmosphere seemed to have changed.

An America newly aware of Hitler's atrocities would be more welcoming. Social advancement seemed possible, and as part of a reverse migration, many second-generation Jews would want to put the Holocaust behind them, strike out and brave the perils of the non-Jewish world for a chance at joining the burgeoning middle class. Leah, a born adventurer, impatient with labels and ghettoes, would be among the assimilationists. Her appetite for freedom included a longing to eat what she wanted (like recidivist dieters, she and Arnold would go on and off keeping Kosher), meet other kinds of people, live a life unrestricted by religious constraints. She would even drop "Leah" for the more ambiguous nickname Lee.

When they moved to New Jersey, Steven would take with him haunting memories, sensations capable of transubstantiation into indelible images. Biographers and reporters have relayed memories Spielberg is said to have had from this period, but it's virtually impossible for a toddler of less than two to form such memories. More likely, his parents told him vivid stories about his early years, and the ones he retained are those that fit in with his emerging storytelling self. This kind of narrative reworking of preverbal sensation provides the double vision of films like the animated movie *An American Tail* and its sequel *Fievel Goes West* in which Holocaust imagery and reverberations play out in a children's story.

Rightly, much has been made of the importance of the recurring light shows in his movies. A "primal scene," cited by biographers as the seed image of his later work, occurred when the six-month-old toddler was taken by his parents to the Adath Synagogue for a service with Hasidic elders and first laid eyes on the Ark of the Torah. He described the dazzling experience—a sudden blast of red light and sound, seemingly of supernatural origin—in a 1985 interview with Richard Corliss of *Time* magazine, as his earliest memory, occurring in 1948.[4] In fact, it would have been 1947, but at the time of the interview Spielberg was still passing off his birth year as 1947. Aware of precocious geniuses like Orson Welles, he'd begun crafting his own legend at an early age. He wanted to direct his first film before he was twenty-one.

Joseph McBride, in his invaluable biography, describes the scene in exquisite detail: Framed by a marble arch, inlaid with gold and blue; a red light burning in front of it, the Ark's wooden doors hidden by a curtain shimmering in candlelight. On high, a bronze chandelier hangs from the domed skylight, and from it a Star of David. All around the elders sway and chant rhythmically.[5]

As beautiful as it sounds to our comprehending minds, it must also have been terrifying to this tiny infant—the sheer hugeness and brightness, the spooky elders, the mournful sounds, all contributing to one of those unbearably intense moments that a child experiences but with no concept, no words, no meaning to tame it. For all we know, that Ark may have triggered a primal anxiety attack, its unappeased fears as crucial to future films as images of transcendence. Think of the lurid spirits that emerge from the coveted Ark at the end of the first Indiana Jones film: rotting fanged creatures who inflict spectacularly hideous deaths on everyone but Indy and Marion.

This little boy, though, seems to have possessed to an extraordinary, even an unsettling degree what scientists describe as emotional memory enhanced by anxiety. The boy in the man, a Proust with a Steadicam, manages to retain the wonder while gaining mastery of the fear. The Ark in its fearful glory will have an amazing plasticity through all his metaphoric reworkings, a call to transcendence that speaks in a universal language to audiences of every nation, tribe, and religion.

2

Steve Bites His Nails and Hears Voices

In 1949, in a move for which Leah (aka Lee) was indirectly responsible, the family relocated to New Jersey, where Arnold had been hired by RCA to work at its manufacturing plant in Camden. Having failed to win a college scholarship after high school, he might never have tried again, but Leah, believing in his talent, had persuaded him to apply to the University of Cincinnati on the G.I. Bill after he finished his military service. He attended night school and won his engineering degree, and now a childhood fascination with mechanics and then electronics was paying off.

Instead of going into television work, as he'd expected, he was assigned to work in military electronics, in circuit development within the new field of computer technology, where transistors were beginning to replace magnetics. His timing was perfect. Because of the heating up of competition with the Soviet Union, the barriers against Jews in science and higher education were falling, and RCA chairman David Sarnoff was one of the few Jews in the upper echelons of business. (Another was the communications mogul William Paley, also of Ukrainian descent.)

It was the postwar Eisenhower years, and everybody had to own a house and a car and a television. In 1949, the Spielbergs got their first television set, and Steven's first sister, Anne, was born on Christmas Day. In 1952, the family moved from Camden to the slightly more upscale suburb of Haddon Township, where they stayed until moving to Arizona in 1957. In both places, Steven would feel like an outsider. It would be worse in echt-suburban Phoenix. But he was already showing plenty of anxiety and nervousness.

Haddon Township was a mixed neighborhood, unlike the adjacent Haddon, which was restricted to gentiles. The township was populated by Protestants, Catholics, and even a few Jews, but his own block—Crystal Terrace—was mostly Christian. Steven was full of mischief and curiosity, but also resentments. He lived in a household of women: his mother held all-women concerts in their living room, and his three sisters—also beneficiaries of Leah's hands-off parenting style—just kept coming and coming. "I had to assert myself," he told Andy Warhol in the 1982 interview (on Warhol's TV show) in which he complained about the dog being female.[1] Like any male outnumbered and on the defensive, he turned torturer, and his favorite prey was, naturally, the opposite sex, starting with his sisters. A favorite trick was to lock them in a closet, then thrust in their faces a plastic skull with a flashlight inside. As he escalated to female targets in the neighborhood, Leah would merely shrug. "His badness was so original," she later said, "there weren't even books to tell you what to do."[2]

He was agitated, energetic, curious, fearful. And he began his lifelong habit of biting his fingernails. He did poorly in school, but was fascinated by radio and television, and not just the content—he would get right up to the tube. He would listen for hours, convinced he heard voices calling to him through the snow or the static. As he related in the Warhol interview, it was one of those auditory phenomena that used to occur in the jumble between competing signals, but he was sure they were sending messages only he could decipher. In *Poltergeist*, which he would produce in 1982, the little girl sits before the TV and hears voices through what the adults see only as snow. Tuned into an alternate universe, she's a little eerie; like other children who crop up in Spielberg films—the possessed kid in the terrifying early TV movie *Something Evil*, Barry in *Close Encounters of the Third Kind*, and culminating in the robot David in *A.I.*—she has an ectoplasmic glow.

He was developing phobias, and collecting a storehouse of fright images. One bête noire was the clutch of maple trees outside his window (it would appear in *Poltergeist*), which on dark and stormy nights became a ghostly hydralike monster, its gnarled branches waving frantically like grasping witch arms. This he would combine or heighten with spooky scene memories from Disney films, in his lifelong talent for turning his own fears into instruments of torture, terrifying audiences with them, much as he had done to his sisters.

His father spent long hours away from the family, and Steven resented it. One day Arnold came home with a transistor. . . . "This is the future," he announced, giving it to Steven . . . who promptly swallowed it. "I was saying that's your future," Spielberg later told *Time* magazine, "but it doesn't have to be mine."[3] Intending to make a gesture of Oedipal defiance, the son was also incorporating into his being, like a communion wafer, the engineering miracle proffered by his father.

It was probably about this time that Steven began casting Arnold as a villain, the Absent Father, the intellectual (or ineffectual) nerd. He could identify with neither of the two men in his life as role models. Arnold was academically inclined, and

Steven hated school. Grandpa Fievel, who would often visit, was an altogether different kind of impossible. For the most part, the Spielbergs seem to have fit in more than Steven remembers. He was a bundle of energy, and if his sadistic tendencies alarmed some parents, he was popular with friends for exploits like the torture chamber he built in the basement. Yet nothing brought home the sense of his own difference like a visit from the Orthodox grandfather. Fievel was the unassimilable Other, bringing the culture of the ghetto with him.

The family was sporadic in its attendance at synagogue, and Spielberg once used the term "storefront kosher" to describe their habit of observing the Jewish dietary laws only when the rabbi or grandparents were visiting. Once, Leah and Steven had to hide the lobsters under the bed. Grandpa Fievel "spoke funny" (according to one neighbor), and, of course, dressed funny. Steven lived in dread of his grandfather suddenly appearing on the porch like an Old Testament prophet and beginning to daven while he was playing with friends. He would pretend he didn't know him.

These ethnic culture shocks would intrude upon the bland conformities of his fifties environment with a double message: you're assimilated, but don't forget you're Jewish. Inside, at his grandfather's knee, he would be entertained and terrified by stories of pogroms: in the dark of the night, a family would awaken to the sound of galloping hoofbeats, dogs barking, and human screams, as fire-breathing Cossacks coursed through the shtetl, torching houses. There was also the legend of how Fievel got his education: in the nineteenth century, czar-imposed quotas limited the number of Jews who could receive higher education. When Fievel wasn't allowed into the secondary school, he found that he could observe from outside the classroom window. This story made the deepest impression on his grandson, whose films would be filled with images of outsiders looking in.

In New Jersey he wanted only to be an insider, denying

his grandfather, as he would deny his Jewishness. "Being a Jew meant that I was not normal," he said. "I was not like everybody else. I just wanted to be accepted. Not for who I was. I wanted to be accepted for who everybody else was."[4]

Steven's sense of anxiety and isolation would reach a crescendo at Christmastime. The holiday's place has evolved as our world has become more secular and our culture has become one of 24/7 consumerism, but for those of us who were children in the forties and fifties, Christmas was the great event of the year. Around the glittering tree consolidated a whole fantasy of the perfect family, belief that our parents would always be there for us. This would have been especially keen in a family that was gradually coming apart: Leah and Arnold were entering a decadelong fight that would be at least as traumatic as the question of religious identity.

Steven was surrounded by emblems of Christianity, like a nativity scene on a neighbor's porch. He was fascinated by rituals and asked lots of questions. His mother told him Christ was not the Messiah, but his friends wondered why he didn't believe or get presents. No doubt at Steven's instigation, the family would drive downtown to see the Christmas decorations and the huge Santa Claus outside the A&P (see the jolly Santa bobbing over the chaos of Los Angeles awaiting a Japanese invasion in his *1941*).

One Christmas, according to an interview he gave Julie Salamon of the *Wall Street Journal*, he decided to create his own religious tableau on the front porch.[5] He ran an extension cord through a window, rigged up a color wheel with gel of different colors, and had his sister Anne, then four, handle the switch. In the middle of the scene stood "Jesus"—Steven draped in white, assuming a Crucifixion pose. When people drove by he would give Anne a signal so that they would see Jesus bathed in a holy light.

His father, when queried by McBride, doubted that his son

would actually have dressed as Jesus, at least in his sight. He would have told him, "You can't do that, we're Jewish."[6] But then he admitted that he could visualize Steven doing it. And so can we.

He couldn't *have* Christmas for himself, but he could "repurpose" it. Consider the otherworldly savior E.T. The blinding light at the door in *Close Encounters of the Third Kind.* What is this sound and light show, this ethereal song, this luminous ship from outer space but a Jewish child's fantasy of Christmas? The Lost Ark.

Knowing of his son's disappointment, Arnold tried to make it up to him. With Spielbergian ingenuity, he cast around, found a candelabra, attached blue bulbs to it, and presto: a menorah! Much as Otto Frank tried to make it up to his daughter Anne, who lamented that "St. Nicholas Day is much more fun than Hanukkah."

He wouldn't be the first Jewish child to cherish Christmas as an all-embracing symbol of American togetherness, a holiday both secular and religious in which all outsiders could become insiders. As Neal Gabler points out in *An Empire of Their Own: How The Jews Invented Hollywood*, it was Irving Berlin, a cantor's son, who wrote "that most Jewish of Yuletide fantasies," "White Christmas."[7] After all, the fantasy of a unified, homogeneous America that dominated films of the classic era came not from the natives, the Wasps who had no need of it, but from the immigrants, principally Jews, whose dream of assimilation led to a kind of superpatriotic vision of America and celebration of its Christian holidays (think *Easter Parade*), to the enshrinement of family and community, an ur-America that, while the dream lasted, glossed over ethnicity and diversity with an inclusive middle-class ideal. Just as this dominant myth was breaking down in the post-fifties, Spielberg would arrive to reinvigorate the fantasy, making films for an "everyone" that we were told no longer existed.

Hanukkah presents itself as a kind of low-rent Christmas in *An American Tail*, an animated film that Spielberg would produce in 1986 about the Mouskewitz family, living in a shtetl in Russia, where pogroms by czarist cats are an everyday occurrence. About to flee Russia for the paradisial (and reportedly cat-free) America, they are celebrating their last Hanukkah, but young son Fievel and his sister Tanya are pulling long faces over their presents: a babushka for her (bo-ring!), for him a blue captain's hat that belonged to his great-grandfather. "Three generations," Papa M says proudly, a legacy that at the moment means little to the son, who had hoped for something shiny and new.

The family emigrates to New York, where, after various misadventures involving felines and felonies, a sequel (*Fievel Goes West*, 1991) takes them from the dirt- and cat-infested tenements of the Bronx to the Wild West, where they've been promised that cats and mice get along. Some years before *Schindler's List*, Spielberg would thus treat the theme of persecution of the Jews through forced emigration, of promises desperately believed and hopes dashed by brutal reality. And with them, the Spielbergian trope of a child's separation from his family.

Often Spielberg expressed parts of himself in films he produced that might be too frightening (*Poltergeist*) or risqué (*Who Framed Roger Rabbit*) for the mainstream audience he sought. And animation provides its own liberation: by translating human behavior into animal behavior, cartoons can perpetrate all sorts of outrages that would be unacceptable in a live-action film. Time can be traveled effortlessly, as when a nineteenth-century mouse migrates into a twentieth-century Western! Women can be sexier, murders more graphic; the animator can change tone abruptly, whisk away trauma with the swipe of a pen.

The assurance of no more cats, and then of congenial ones,

would be recognized as empty promises—by children because where there are mice there are predatory cats, and by adults because of all too familiar histories of persecution and genocide. *Fievel Goes West* provides another stunning example of this layered approach when the mice are transported to "Green River." Anticipating the transit trucks in *Schindler's List*, the trip initially seems a glorious adventure, the green and yellow train, seen from on high, chugging through the heartland of America, Western music a-strumming, the landscape dotted by wedges of cheese. But it suddenly turns ominous when Fievel overhears Cat-o-Waul, the feline ringleader, lay out the plan to his gang of ravenous poker-playing cats. When Fievel returns to his family, the cattle car is framed as a cramped space, a huge chain running beneath it, the music obliterated by the rattling of the train, now a dark silhouette against the midnight blue sky.

Adults would experience a shudder of recognition at the trains hurtling unsuspecting passengers toward the unknown, while the death camp implications would go over the heads of children, who would respond to the scary adventures and comic juxtapositions.

The two-part Fievel saga is in many ways more deeply personal than 1993's *Schindler's List*, the film that certified the director's rebirth as a Jew, and his much-vaunted evolution into a newfound "maturity" as a man and a director. At one point in the planning stage, Don Bluth, the ex-Disney animator who directed the second film, suggested they change Fievel's name into something less ethnic, but Spielberg refused.

Some people object to *American Tail* as a sentimental treatment of this darkest of themes. Art Spiegelman, who was publishing his graphic masterpiece *Maus* in *Raw* magazine at the same time he and Bluth were at the School of Visual Arts, suspected that his idea was being "recuperated" into a commercial film. In a documentary about him by Clara and Julia Kuperberg, he told the filmmakers he was even afraid that people would confuse his name with Spielberg's. In fact, each man became a celebrity in his own right, and anyone who refers to "Mouse" among the culturally savvy is thinking of *Maus*.

In any case, rodent protagonists are animation favorites, more often victims than predators. Stuart Little, Mickey, Ratatouille. Each mouse is distinctive, with little graphic resemblance. *Maus* is about a son's bridging the gap between himself and his survivor father by persuading him to tell him stories of Poland and the ordeal of the concentration camp. Fievel is definitely closer to Disney than to Dachau, but that doesn't make his tale anodyne. If anything, he most resembles Amos in Disney's 1953 two-reeler *Ben and Me*, in which the poor little mouse from a "downtrodden race" leaves his impoverished family to seek work, and winds up assisting Ben Franklin with his inventions and Thomas Jefferson with the writing of the Declaration of Independence. Spielberg's cartoon is founded on the American idea of assimilating and rising, but infused with a certain outsider ambivalence.

Nineteen eighty-six, when *An America Tail* was made, was a moment of immigrant influx. The United States had made a deal with the Soviet Union to trade, as Gary Shteyngart put it, wheat for Jews. The portrait the films paint is hardly an encomium to the Statue of Liberty. The anguish is over lost family and continued persecution. The politics and class issues are local, the references are sketched with subtlety and sophistication. What makes the films Spielbergian is the way he folds the family story with its ethnic roots into the universal story of a boy coming of age in America. In part one, he grows into his captain's hat. In part two, he exchanges it, when action leadership is needed, for a ten-gallon hat.

He would not be the first Jew to want to be a cowboy, or to be drawn to the American Southwest. Art Spiegelman, when asked how he came by his profession, admits that he became a cartoonist when he realized he couldn't be a cowboy. Think of other urban émigrés: Billy Crystal on a cattle ranch in *City Slickers* (1991), not to mention the Gene Wilder–Cleavon Little duo staring down the bad guys in Mel Brooks's Yiddish-black *Blazing Saddles* (1974).

In becoming a director, Spielberg would get to play vicariously and imaginatively all the roles denied him and other Jews not just in life but on the Hollywood screen. A yearning for American-style heroism impels Fievel to emulate his idol, the sheriff—played by Jimmy Stewart in his last screen role. Fievel becomes a hero with a Jewish twist: he's the one who warns of impending doom, the one to whom nobody listens.

3

Arcadia: The Best and Worst of Times

If he felt like an outsider in New Jersey, he would feel like an extraterrestrial in Arizona, living in a Phoenix suburb on the fringe of the desert. Over the course of thirteen years, he lived in three different places, but he considered Scottsdale, where he lived from age nine to sixteen, his real home. The Spielbergs bought a ranch house in a brand new and upwardly mobile development called Arcadia, as middle-American as you could get and anchored in all the unthinking bigotries of the fifties. Women hadn't begun to shed their Donna Reed aprons and deconstruct the Feminine Mystique, except for one notoriously nonconformist "Lee," who, for all her assimilationist fervor, was nonplussed by the sheer conventionality of the place.

It was, Spielberg would recall, just like the neighborhood in *Poltergeist:* "kitchen windows facing kitchen windows facing kitchen windows. People would wave to each other from their windows." For the ten-year-old, a treasure chest of images:

bland surfaces that spoke of conformity and repression, the chockablock sameness of the development against the generously unpeopled vistas and vast night skies at the foot of Camelback Mountain.

If Arizona was the best as well as the worst of places and times for Steven, it represented on the debit side another uprooting, another school where he had to make new friends while enduring the social and hormonal upheaval of being a teenager. He felt more like an outsider than ever, "a wimp in a world of jocks." His ears stuck out, his nose was too long. Bullies called him "Spielbug."

He went through what he called a six-month period as a juvenile delinquent, which included terrorizing his sisters in ever more inventive ways and misbehaving at his bar mitzvah (he went up on the roof and pelted guests below with oranges). By now, the friction between Arnold and Leah had erupted into a nonstop war. As Spielberg recounted it years later, Leah would be playing the piano in one room with a coven of female friends, while in another, Arnold was hunched over with fellow engineers, discussing "a computer mousetrap."[1] The boy would seal himself into his room, stuffing a towel under the door to shut out the noise.

But if Arizona was the social and emotional nadir, it was also where he found his métier, and with it, a growing confidence that helped allay the domestic turmoil and feelings of inadequacy. With a camera in hand, he could not only shut out all the horrors that swirled around him, he could tackle one of them—unpopularity—in his own way.

Arnold lent Steven a Brownie, his first, then gave him an 8 millimeter camera he'd received from a friend. Arnold had always taken the family movies when they went on vacation, but as soon as he showed his son how to use it, Steven, by Arnold's own account, leaped past his father as a videographer, immediately forgoing the stodgy newsreel style of the home movie genre to reshape, even re-create, reality. He would film the family arriving in a car, shooting from an oblique angle ("from the hubcap" Leah remembered), then, if he wasn't satisfied, make them do it all over again. "Staging real life was so much more fun than just recording it," he remembered.[2]

As a budding filmmaker, he was dealing in action and "special effects" from the start, his chief protagonist being his electric train, and his preferred action mode being the train wreck. He was making silent movies, learning by instinct how to create excitement through cutting and tempo and close-ups, his forte being explosions and pileups. Perhaps these also provided an outlet for the rage and free-floating anxiety caused by the friction between his parents. Adding to the tension, his father, a child of the Depression, was constantly badgering him to use less film, which was quite expensive: thus he and Arnold entered into that other fractious dynamic, that of the director and his producer.

There were numerous picnics and camping expeditions, and the vast spaces of Arizona would come to occupy an almost holy place in Steven's visual repertoire. He had been bowled over when he got his first glimpse of the skies through a telescope kept by his scoutmaster, Uncle Buddy, in his backyard. And his mind was permanently blown into the stratosphere of science fiction when, at the age of ten, he went with his father to *Destination Moon*, about a rocket voyage. Forever after, and through all the trials at home and school, outer space would be both a refuge and a theater for his fantasies.

Once Arnold woke him up in the middle of the night, put him in the car, and without telling him where they were going, drove into the desert. Arnold had brought along a thermos of coffee. Where was Leah? Steven was scared. (Was his father kidnapping him?) They got out, lay on a blanket, looked up at the sky, so clear and free of smog that the stars seemed larger and closer than they'd ever been. Finally, Arnold told him they were there because he'd read that a comet was supposed to appear at a certain time. What happened instead was a meteor shower. The brightness and intensity of the falling stars disconcerted Arnold, who tried to explain it scientifically, but Steven, no longer frightened, was enraptured by the magnificence of the falling stars. His original fear of domestic upheaval evaporated; everything was all right, more than all right. An aficionado of *The Twilight Zone*, and its promise of a fourth dimension, Steven simply luxuriated in this celestial wonder.

His reshaping memory was already at work: years later, elements of the heavenly shower would crop up in *Close Encounters of the Third Kind*. Another primal "Christmas" scene, a child awakened in the night, is led shivering and blindfolded to the "tree" with the stars laid out like presents from the Almighty. When he came to use the incident, instead of just father and son, the scene would expand to include hundreds of people on blankets searching the skies for a UFO. Just as crucial is its dark underside and more sinister counterpart, the initial fear, the possible kidnapping of a child, which crops up again and again in Spielberg films.

The embryonic action and science fiction filmmaker was ready to showcase his talent for an audience. Success would come when he became a Boy Scout, joining an institution that would hold a deeply cherished place for him all his life. As a member of the Flaming Arrow Patrol of Ingleside's Troop 294, he wasn't good at the usual feats of physical dexterity that earned merit badges, so Arnold suggested that he go for the photography badge by making a film. The result was a nine-minute Western called *Gunfight*.

He had already learned that he could entertain fellow members with his stories around the campfire (his were the best and scariest); now he would wow them with his movies. His film was ecstatically received. From then on, he would take his camera on expeditions and film the other boys, to their delight. The Boy Scouts filled a vacuum, social, emotional, and quasi-religious. He discovered the male bonding and mentorship he felt Arnold had denied him, and he became part of an institution, a sort of congregation he hadn't yet found in Judaism. He had gone to Hebrew school, which he hated, and had acted out his rejection of his Jewish identity at his bar mitzvah. It was with the Boy Scouts that, for the first time, he felt a sense of belonging.

After *Gunfight*, his first story film, would come fiction films of increasing length and ambition. When he wanted to make a Western, Arnold would take the crew—Boy Scouts and neighborhood kids—to a restaurant that had a stagecoach out front. Steven had always been fascinated by World War II and his dad's experiences in the army. Arnold had enlisted in 1942, then been transferred to the Army Air Forces as a radio operator and seen some action in Southeast Asia. But because of the high value placed on his technological expertise, he'd spent most of the time until his discharge in the squadron's communications room.

Arnold also helped his son get permits for his movies and arranged for him to use a real plane for a World War II film, *Fighter Squad*, begun in the seventh grade—an action film about G.I.'s escaping from a German fighter squad, using the plane mixed with stock footage.

What was remarkable, according to all who knew him, was the focus and intensity Steven displayed, the absolute confidence on the "set," how coolly he went about telling his "cast" and "crew" (family and friends) what to do.

There would be girls, but mostly as friends. Some remembered him as being shy but friendlier than some of the boys. Where they would torment girls and tie them to trees (a behavior Steven reserved for his little sisters and younger girls), he would feature his favorite girls in 8 mm movies.

Steven's already timid relationship with the opposite sex would be shocked into inertia by the consequences of his first date. In the fifth grade, according to Steven's later telling, he had a crush on a girl, and Arnold took the two to a drive-in. At some point, the girl put her head on his arm. When he got home, Arnold reported the incident to Leah, and there was hell to pay. "Promiscuous" was the word they used. This scared him off girls, or at least served as a good reason to stay clear of entanglements. Afterward, he rarely dated: he didn't have time and he needed to save money for film.

He now expanded his areas of expertise and became an exhibitor, publicist, and pollster. He got 16 mm Disney films available for nonprofit showings, promoted them with flyers and posters he and Arnold made, then ran them for neighborhood kids in the Spielberg family room. He would also occasionally throw in his own films as curtain raisers, like *A Day in the Life of Thunder*, which featured his cocker spaniel ambling around the neighborhood all day, his leash harnessed to a camera on a cart—*Lawrence of Arcadia?*

After showings of a movie like *Davy Crockett: King of the Wild Frontier*, he'd conduct his own focus group, quizzing the audience on its likes and dislikes. He also began his future career as a philanthropist. He charged admission, planning to buy more film with the money, but Arnold suggested he'd get a lot more credit and goodwill if he gave it to charity. He therefore donated his first profits to the Perry Institute Home for Mentally Handicapped Children, a cause—children's health and welfare—that would become a lifelong commitment.

As prelude to his shrewd sense of ancillary profits and diversification, he did keep the proceeds from the "concession stand" run by his sisters at the home screenings, giving them a percentage. And he did other odd jobs for neighbors to get money for films. All of his activities, day and night, were directed toward film—buying film, planning films, making them. Even at so young an age, he was driven, as if time were running out.

When not at school or skipping school to make movies, he was reading science fiction, watching television, or going to the movies. Arnold took him and another boy to see *Psycho* at the drive-in, and all three were terrified. In the backyard, he and a friend put together a silent, two-reel Western homage to John Ford's *The Searchers.*

There are conflicting stories, including his own, about how much or how little he watched television. When he was small, certain programs so terrified him that Arnold rigged the set with a booby trap—making it more desirable, of course. Later, Steven said his television diet was severely restricted, but the many references in his films and interviews indicate that this wasn't true. Probably the Spielbergs simply looked down on television as trash and, like most families in that quaint era of parental authority, tried to limit the viewing hours. But the guilty feeling that something he instinctively loved was considered culturally inferior would have fed both the guilt (a betrayal of those higher ambitions fostered by Arnold) and the perverse longing to make just that kind of fare.

This was the height of his animus toward his father, whom he needed to blame for everything—for being absent, for being too strict. At this point, according to a friend, he was totally his mother's child, and embittered about his father to the point that he "disowned" him. Seeing Arnold's enthusiastic involvement with his son's movie activities makes us wonder about Steven's deep and abiding anger at his father. But Arnold wasn't casually nurturing, didn't hang out with the boy and play catch. And even more important, he was a classic "brain," a fifties high achiever, successful in the sort of intellectual pursuits at which Steven could never excel. Steven constantly felt his father's disappointment, a blight over his young life. His inventiveness and imagination counted for nothing in the scale of things, were even a handicap to seriousness. Television to the rescue, as a "stepparent" and an act of low-culture defiance that stimulated and comforted him and brought order in the midst of confusion.

Arnold's intellectualism was synonymous with "wimp," which in turn seemed equated with Jewishness: tormenters often conflated the two. So he would identify with the non-Jewish philistines and jocks and turn the Jewish Holy Grail—intellectual achievement—into an object of scorn. Hence the ambivalence bordering on contempt for the boy in *Amblin'*, the Steven surrogate, who, as it happens, was played by a librarian. According to biographer Joseph McBride, Spielberg once said he wanted to be a gentile with the same intensity that he wanted to be a filmmaker.[3]

Despite the tensions between father and son over grades, academic commitment, the baleful influence of television, they had much in common. Arnold would share with Steven his fascination with science fiction, and would tell stories about going to the movies as a kid and loving Douglas Fairbanks in swashbuckling adventures like *The Thief of Baghdad.* Even the interest in technology—he actually made a television set in the 1950s, as well as bringing home that transistor—was something Steven shared, though from a different perspective.

Arnold's sin of absenteeism was the pattern of so many suburban dads, trying to provide for a growing family, working longer hours for ever-increasing paychecks and nicer houses. But his absences did mean that, given Leah's permissiveness, there was no adult figure on the scene. And Steven was at an age when he needed discipline, even conventionality.

Like one of those notorious mother-son outlaw pairs, she was his partner in crime, even his Lady Macbeth. She drove the jeep on scouting expeditions, she told Ed Bradley on *60 Minutes* in 1993, and "wrote notes to teachers. . . . I loved to keep him home. I had a pith helmet and fatigues and would drive him out into the desert."[4]

Neighbors in Arizona thought Leah decidedly odd, especially as she was often seen with Bernie, the couple's best friend. It was, of course, only years later, when Leah was on the point of remarrying, that Steven would learn that his mother had fallen for their "Uncle Bernie." What were the children to make of Uncle Bernie and the morality of this Orthodox Jew?

Leah never denied the affair. "I was smitten," she would say. "I was madly in love."

Leah's nonconformism, her bohemian reputation, had begun to embarrass him. Now he longed for a mother who played bridge and attended PTA meetings like the other mothers. "The conventional always appealed to Steven," she told an interviewer, "maybe because we weren't."[5]

The next cinematic coup was *Fighter Squad*, begun in 1959 and completed and shown in 1962 to prizes and acclaim. Shot with six cameras, incorporating stock footage, and using the actual plane that Arnold had somehow managed to obtain, the movie was a dazzling action display. If the characters were less than skin deep, they served a useful purpose: as an early example of his curiosity about the enemy Other, he himself played the Nazi villain, and he found a part for one of the guys who'd bullied him, thus co-opting him forever. Though he fared poorly in schoolyard combat, he'd learned how to disarm the enemy without use of force.

All the emotional undercurrents in his life—the family tensions and his own restless search for identity—only intensified after he graduated from elementary school and went to Arcadia High, a huge, state-of-the-art school that was more conservative, more upper-middle-class, than Ingleside. But it was where he also found kindred souls, creative weirdos like himself, and even formed a circle of friends. As in most suburban high schools, athletics were paramount. But there were Jews in the student body mix; there were top-flight facilities, including a drama club and a band, both of which he joined. He still saw arty enterprises like the drama club from the jocks' point of view, calling it "the leper colony." He tried acting, but was shy and awkward, couldn't remember his lines (a liability that would enable him to identify with actors in later years), and stumbled in reading and did poorly in school. Because of his habit of faking illness to stay home and work on his movies, he was often subject to disciplinary action. His weak academic performance and a lack of interest in going to college—unique among this fairly elite student body—caused friction with Arnold, who was pressuring him to become a doctor or an electrical engineer.

Nevertheless he and Leah got behind *Firelight*, Steven's first feature film, about a UFO. He had won a 16 mm camera as a prize, but Arnold convinced him to trade it in for an 8 millimeter, the Bolex Sonerizer, so that he could record direct sound for the first time. He used the Bolex to make a film inspired by the UFO he and Arnie *didn't* see that memorable night under the stars. Like most growing up in the fifties, he was fascinated by reports of flying saucers and stories of life forms on other planets.

It was like a dry run for *Close Encounters* and *E.T.*, with alien invaders, a fragile home life, an isolated youngster. The difference is that the tropes in *Firelight* are more conventionally fifties sci-fi than Spielbergian, with menacing aliens who threaten to take over the minds of humans, and paranoia toward both the government and the extraterrestrials.

There are also echoes of *The Twilight Zone* and an obsessed UFO expert. The scientist is both "mad" and right—in other words, a man who warns but to whom nobody listens. This Cassandra-like figure—truth teller or madman, prophet of the apocalypse to an unbelieving world—serves as an archetype in several twentieth-century narratives: in science fiction, the seer who foretells the extinction of man, but also the lone Jew who sees where the cattle cars are headed in Poland and Germany.

The young director deployed family and pets as dramatis personae: a dog is abducted, and later a little girl, played by one of Spielberg's sisters, disappears, thus (Freudian alert!) causing her mother to die of a heart attack. Evil or the Otherworldly Other responsible for these suburban catastrophes emanates from a red light, the "Master Image," and an instinctual blend of the fearful and the wondrous.

Arnold and Leah were heading toward divorce; the breakup of the marriage was much on Steven's mind, and of course figures in the story. The movie tells of a marriage in trouble—only of course it's the *husband* who has an eye for another man's wife. Maybe just as loaded with meaning is the timing of that ominous light, which first appears to a boy and girl in a car, a couple obviously on their first date. She has her head on his shoulder when they witness the flash. Immobilized with fear, she screams before a further transgression can be committed.

As designed by Spielberg with Arnold's help, *Firelight* was an incredibly complex undertaking. He wrote a sixty-seven-page screenplay, and for his first original soundtrack, he used the high school band to play a score that he wrote. (He was always musical and an avid record collector. In later years, his longtime composer John Williams would say Spielberg himself could have been a composer.) He played clarinet and Leah the piano. He worked out a host of ingenious visual effects in the Spielberg carport, which was also the studio, while location shooting took place around Phoenix and Camelback Mountain.

The acting and dialogue may have been amateurish, the script full of hoary rhetoric, but the storytelling was visually inventive, and Spielberg already showed a masterly ability to orchestrate complex movements. People on the set marveled at both his know-how in performing every facet of filmmaking and the childlike joy with which he did it. Someone who had been with him when he made *Fighter Squad* said, "He was one of the least childish fourteen year olds I have ever seen."[6]

Yet in other ways, he was very much a child. As with that other archetypal twentieth-century genius-nerd in the garage also named Steve, Spielberg's technical and problem-solving skills evolved exponentially, at the expense of his emotional and social side. There would be other points of comparison with Jobs. In redrawing the cultural map, both showmen would run enterprises that were more collective than individual, both would have plenty of help, perhaps more than was ever officially acknowledged. Yet each was a magician—and a salesman of magic—with a powerful personal vision and mastery of style that subsumed, molded, streamlined, and blended the work of others.[7]

It's the peculiarities of the two childhoods that make all the difference: the inventor of Mac and the iPhone never recovered from the fact of his adoption, and was to all appearances incapable of genuine family feeling; he invented a futuristic gadget that would enable us all to be alone together. The little prince Spielberg, on the other hand, was loved to distraction. The parental battles, however searing, were cushioned by adoration, and the ominous rumbles of divorce just made him that much more appreciative of what he was about to lose. Jobs's inventions, his manic workaholism, were all an escape from domesticity. Spielberg, by contrast, would place home life at the center; even the future would become family friendly.

On March 24, 1964, *Firelight* had its grand premiere at a Phoenix theater, complete with searchlights, limousine (carrying the director and his stars), flashbulbs, and reviews. His proud mother called her precocious seventeen-year-old son Cecil B. DeSpielberg. The movie cost less than six hundred dollars, and at seventy-five cents a head, it made a small profit.

4

The Kid with the Briefcase

IT WAS THE summer of 1964. His family had been relocated to Silicon Valley, where his father, now in the new field of computer processing, had been recruited for a top job at the IBM plant in San Jose. Another upscale move, this time to Saratoga, a rich, ultraconservative resort town in the foothills of the Santa Cruz Mountains. It was here that Steven would finish his last year of high school, and his parents would finally end the marriage to whose shreds they had mysteriously clung for ten embattled years. It was a year of misery redeemed by tiny but surefooted steps forward on the path to a professional career.

Over the years reporters heard a number of versions of how he "broke into" the film business; Spielberg was as cunning at crafting his own legend as he was at every other aspect of his career. At the fanciful end of the spectrum was the stealth invasion of Universal Studios: he was taking a tour his last summer of high school, when he jumped off the bus, sneaked inside, found an empty office with a telephone, and, like Eloise at the Plaza, made himself at home.

He did eventually have access to an office and a phone, but it came about rather more conventionally, through an interview set up by a family friend, with Chuck Silvers of the Universal editorial department. Silvers, the first of his mentors at Universal, was reorganizing the studio's film library, while Steven was taking a break and completing postproduction on *Firelight.* As the two chatted about films, Silvers was impressed by the kid's knowledge and enthusiasm, and arranged for him to get a pass—a one-day pass that Steven somehow managed to extend so that, as Silvers told McBride, he "was able to walk onto the lot just about any time he damn well pleased."[1] Silvers found him an office he could share with Julie Raymond, the television editorial department's purchasing agent, and some clerical work that didn't involve the union. In return, he would be a "guest apprentice," given free range of the studio. While his future colleagues were attending film school, he was designing his own curriculum, learning the craft.

"Every day for three months in a row," he told the *Hollywood Reporter,* "I walked through the gates dressed in a sincere black suit and carrying a briefcase. I visited every set I could, got to know people, observed techniques, and just generally absorbed the atmosphere."[2]

He figured people would take him for the son of one of the executives in the Black Tower. It was still a "middle-aged man's profession," and one, he quickly realized, that wasn't about to welcome him with open arms. He was trying for the first and last time to pass as a grown-up, but he was also the thin wedge in the door of the youthful army mustering at the gates of even the most traditional Hollywood studios. Twenty years later, the kid with the briefcase skulking past the uniformed guard would have his own production company, Amblin, occupying lavish quarters within the same studio precincts—a four- to six-million-dollar "gift" from Universal that was both studio and pleasure dome.

When he wasn't helping Julie, he wandered the back lot, watched films being shot, hung out in the editing room, sometimes making a nuisance of himself, but absorbing whatever he could. He wanted to meet stars, would invite the likes of Charlton Heston and Cary Grant to lunch in the commissary. Some accepted, some didn't; some directors let him watch the shooting, some kicked him off the set. He had charm, chutzpah, and—crucial to his future profession—an inability to be discouraged by a "no."

When he went to Saratoga High School for his senior year, the school paper, with a little P. T. Barnum hyperbole, reported that "Steve Spielberg worked with Hollywood directors this summer at Universal Pictures."

But the headline and the apprenticeship were about the only rays of light in a year of deep unhappiness. Saratoga represented yet another move, another disruption, with all the anxiety of having to make new friends. It was also when his twin demons—antisemitic bullying and the noisy and prolonged breakup of his parents—became both unbearable and indistinguishable.

His friends of the time disagreed about the extent of the antisemitism he faced. Don Schull, his next door neighbor in Saratoga, didn't notice the antisemitism, but then Schull was a big guy, the kind of imposing teenager who would shield Spielberg from the bullies, in whose presence they would simply disappear. Another friend, Gene Ward Smith, intellectual and self-proclaimed fellow nerd, identified with Spielberg's insecurities, and witnessed the persecution. When Steven, always angling to be one of the guys, became a reporter for the school paper, he began covering—of all things—sports. Smith thought it a kind of betrayal of the non-jocks, but also realized how deeply Steven needed to feel a part of the group. He was not quite a pariah, but he was, as he would later express it, "caught in the shadows between the popular kids and the outcasts"—a place alive with pitfalls and possibilities. Mirroring the not-quite-one-thing-or-the-other status of his parents' marriage, he was caught in the middle, close enough to the mainstream to yearn for it. Becoming a sports reporter was one port of entry. With his early and uncanny sense of vocation, perhaps he was instinctively trying to acquire the different kinds of knowledge he would need.

It was Steven who constantly brought up the subject of his Jewishness: what did it mean? He was having trouble squaring Jewishness with his parents' behavior: they claimed to be Jewish but didn't worship or observe its tenets in their daily life.

"You want to know what it means to be Jewish?" he asked Mike Augustine, a friend he had brought home one day when his parents were at it as usual. "That's what it's like to be Jewish—you have an extra glass of wine a day so you can yell louder at one another."[3] (An interesting conflation, as it's usually inhibited Wasps who are associated with imbibing and release.) Augustine's take was that even though Steven's parents were ending their marriage, they were "still devoted to one another." Thus adding an extra layer of emotional complication for the child.

Steven's anger, though personal and very much his own, would also dovetail with the wave of rebellion "without a cause" that inflamed so many teenagers against their parents in the fifties and sixties. Children began questioning parental authority, charging them with hypocrisy. The surface of virtuous appearances—faith, monogamy, loyalty—was cracking. But the so-called hypocrisy was itself a function of a culture in which marriage was forever, divorce was exceedingly rare, and couples stayed together "for the children." Because of the instability of hope raised and then deferred, this kind of ongoing tension can be worse than an out-and-out break. Parents fought quietly and tried to keep their differences secret, but the children sensed conflict and, not understanding it, often blamed themselves.

One escape from the difficulties of sorting out his confusion over his Jewish identity, both rejecting and pursuing it, was Steven's uncomplicated and visceral connection to another history: that of movies, of Hollywood directors. He told Smith, a math brain who was a snob for European films, that American directors were the artists to watch, especially Ford and Hitchcock. What Spielberg loved about Hitchcock after seeing *Psycho* was his indirection, the power of suggestion; his other attraction was his mass appeal. In talks with Smith, he was also developing a more refined taste in science fiction, turning to authors like Heinlein, Asimov, Clarke, and Bradbury.

In the tumultuous early sixties, he might not take to the barricades, but Steven was deeply affected by social events that were going on around him. He was shaken by the Kennedy assassination, and shared with his fellow boomers an awareness of racial discrimination and a growing disillusionment with his country. The personal really was political, as the breakdown in parental authority coincided with, and mirrored, that of America—the "system." Even as he persisted in asking Why were Jews persecuted? he began to make a connection between blacks and Jews as twin victims of prejudice and persecution.

He and Mike Augustine had long discussions of race, of counterculture; they played Lenny Bruce albums and read *Mad* magazine. Often in his life he seems to have had a pal like Mike, who was a little more far out and politically aware than he was, pulling him toward the cutting edge. Now, through Lenny Bruce, Steven began to understand the defensive power of Jewish humor; he and Augustine would take turns playing Jew and Nazi. One of the sources of his distress over the persecutions he had endured was shame for not having fought back; he felt like a coward and realized that humor was both weapon and compensation.

He was also against the Vietnam War, both ideologically and practically: he was graduating, and he had to go to college or be drafted. With his poor academic record his only choice was California State College at Long Beach. It had no film department, but was located within easy driving distance of Universal, so that would become his unofficial university. Neither Leah nor Arnold was pleased, but they were busy with their divorce and had to more or less give Steven free rein.

In the separation agreement, the girls would stay with Leah, and Steve would live with Arnold. At this point, Spielberg blamed the breakup on Leah and would enjoy a brief period of bonding with his father. But his anxiety about the future was intense, and the summary manner in which his parents settled his fate seems to have rankled for years, and would turn up in the expulsion from paradise of Frank Abagnale Jr. (Leonardo DiCaprio) in *Catch Me If You Can.* The feeling of emotional fragility, as well as a need to avoid the draft, sent him into psychotherapy. As he told it, he spent fifty dollars a week telling the analyst stories, stories that were film scripts in the making. He was weaving his personal hang-ups into narratives, practicing the art-as-therapy (and therapy-as-art) that came naturally.

Father and son togetherness ended abruptly when Steven stopped going to classes. Mostly, he used Arnold's apartment as a crash pad while he pursued his plans to enter the film industry. There was a showdown. Later Spielberg would say he wished he'd finished and gotten a degree, but at the time he was a young man in a hurry. Arnold tried to enlist Chuck Silvers in his campaign to keep the boy in college, but Silvers, though he sympathized with Arnold's point, felt his loyalty was to Steven.

Even Leah, the delinquent enabler, was alarmed. He was good in English and at writing . . . but he didn't have the patience to read. He was quick-witted and articulate, a guy who could talk his way into and out of situations. Arnold, fed up, simply kicked him out, whereupon he joined a fraternity, the Theta Chi, significantly not a Jewish one. His new hippie pal and roommate, Ralph Burris, said Steven was straitlaced and driven, that he never drank or used drugs. In 1967 the two moved into a house in the Palms section of West LA and continued living together in the area until Spielberg bought his first house in 1971. There were parties, and there were girls in and out, but not his. Burris was busy being a goof-off, while Spielberg went his own focused way, catching up on movies, devouring knowledge, expertise. He again went to acting classes, joined a film society run by Universal's film buffs. For the first time he saw foreign films, which were showing everywhere in both new releases and retrospectives, and were an education in themselves, even if it wasn't his own preferred school. He hung out with editors, picked up lessons in acting by watching John Cassavetes making *Faces.*

At Universal, still under Chuck Silvers's mentorship, he was learning to adapt to the very system that renegade pals at Nicholas Beach like Coppola and Scorsese were trying to overthrow—or at least co-opt. Universal was the last of the old-fashioned studios, not yet shaken by the forces that were unsettling the country and the other studios. Steven wasn't one of what *Time* in 1968 dubbed "The Student Movie Makers," turning to films as artistic means of expression. He was indeed one of the "movie brats" (another recent coinage), but he was enlisted neither at USC with the "USC Mafia," John Milius and Robert Zemeckis among them, who were trying to be as professional as possible, nor with the "funkier" UCLA guys—Coppola, Paul Schrader, and Carroll Ballard—who were more personal in their approach. After starting to make a film about high-speed bicycle racing called *Slipstream* (he ran out of money before completing it), he told a student reporter, "I don't want to make films like Antonioni or Fellini. I don't want just the elite. I want everybody to enjoy my films." He went on to say, in what was a filmmaking credo both modest and ambitious, that he did want his films to have a purpose, to "say something," but it had to be something meaningful to him that he could convey to an audience. "If, in doing so, I create a style, then that's my style. I'm trying to be original, but originality tends to become stylized. . . . The worst thing for me to do at twenty is to develop a style."[4]

One day Spielberg went to UCLA and was severely jolted when he saw George Lucas's graduate thesis film, *THX 1138* (which would become a theatrical feature three years later). A kid his own age had accomplished more than he had, but he was also excited to find this new mentor.

It was at this juncture that Julie Raymond, his office mate of the previous summer, put him in touch with Denis Hoffman, who wanted to produce and put up $15,000. Together Hoffman and Steven would make *Amblin'*—the calling card that opened doors. Julie got him an editing room, and they shot in the grueling heat of the desert, with no one getting paid, just working for screen credit. The movie would be a showcase for all of them, especially Spielberg. Hoffman would complain, as did others through the years, that Spielberg hadn't given him enough credit, and in 1995 would sue Spielberg for failing to fulfill a multiple-film contract.

A precocious display of moviemaking skills all the more impressive for its tiny budget, *Amblin'* tells an O. Henry–esque story of two hitchhikers, a boy and a girl, who meet heading west on a desert highway and join forces. The boy (Richard Levin, a librarian in real life), dark-skinned and furtive, is loping along with guitar case and duffel bag, and seems a little lost. The girl (Pamela McMyler), long hair swinging, antic and competitive, is the adventurous one and quickly assumes dominance, out-expectorating the boy in a spitball contest. In the darkness of a cave, where they are framed, John Ford–style, against the bright outdoors, she introduces him to pot . . . and then—it would seem—to sex. I say "it would seem," because night has fallen and the shot is in the shadows, obscurely (tactfully?) ambiguous.

Their odyssey, accompanied by riffs on Leone/Morricone and Sergeant Pepper, and guitar thrums keyed to the boy's baggage, features the alterations in scale that would become a hallmark of Spielberg visual storytelling: the aerial point of view, whereby two tiny figures are reduced to precarious dots in a vast landscape; then the camera moving in for the humanizing close-up. Eventually, the couple arrives at the Pacific coast. The boy, yelping with delight, rushes into the ocean. The girl, sitting on the beach, eyes the guitar and, unable to resist any longer, opens the case. Out of it spill Oxford shoes, a striped tie, a roll of toilet paper, mouthwash—the accessories of ambition—along with a book, Arthur C. Clarke's *The City and the Stars*, a lovely pun of a reference: a tribute to the great science fiction writer, but a title that might suggest a guidebook to LA and the homes of celebrities. The guitar case could have been a stand-in for the briefcase that Steven required for his days impersonating an executive's son at the entrance to Universal Studios.

Later, Spielberg would dismiss the film as indifferent to the politics of the time. But the movie displayed something other and more surprising than political engagement: a perspective on the cultural divides that, unlike the more leftish movies being made at the time, didn't take sides. To the extent that it did, the target was the square but ambitious Spielberg surrogate. It was a "youth" movie that the brass at Universal could understand.

His friend and advocate Chuck Silvers was so impressed with the film that he sent it over to Sidney Sheinberg, Universal's vice president in charge of television, and insisted that he watch it immediately. Sheinberg did, called the kid into his office, and offered him a seven-year contract. *Amblin'* would play at various festivals, and after winning a prize at one, it was submitted for Oscar consideration as a live action short, but—in an irony reflecting the divided soul of Hollywood—it was rejected because of the depiction of drugs.

When Spielberg signed with Universal Television, he was twenty-one. He had wanted to make his first feature film by that age, or at least by twenty-five—Orson Welles's age when he made *Citizen Kane*. Welles was a prodigy with a remarkably similar genetic background to Steven's: his mother was a concert pianist, his father an inventor. And there was something about the largeness of Welles, the outsize shadow he cast on popular culture, that made him a yardstick by which Steven needed to measure himself. He ultimately lost the youth race, directing his first feature, *The Sugarland Express*, at twenty-seven, but he established a record as the youngest to sign a long-term contract with a studio.

Silvers and others advised him against boxing himself in with the long-term contract, but he wanted the security. Besides, it sounded like a dream come true, a chance to show people what he could do. In the event, television both was and wasn't an ideal testing ground. The downsides were numerous: long fallow periods between assignments, the straitjacket constraints of shooting for television. "I had more fun making 8 millimeter films as a kid than working in television," he would say, though admitting that the discipline served him well.

As a film stock profligate, he was constantly shooting more film than was acceptable, orchestrating more elaborate setups than was customary, fussing over the editing till they kicked him out of the editing room. He got the reputation of being avant-garde, arty—in other words, difficult. Diva directors weren't unknown in television: Spielberg was a Boy Scout compared to the cantankerous Robert Altman, who had both chafed and experimented at Universal.

His youthful appearance raised eyebrows and concerns from the mostly middle-aged crew and actors, and the diva in the drama wasn't Spielberg but Joan Crawford. Indeed, his first assignment was so terrifying that he almost took to drink—directing an episode of *Night Gallery* with a Crawford who was herself insecure: a neophyte in television, losing her looks and memory, unable to remember her lines or pronounce words like "transcendental" and "esophagus."

Bette Davis had walked off the project when she found it would be directed by a twenty-two-year old, but Crawford accepted Spielberg as a pro, apparently recognizing in him a similarly ambitious self-starter. Improbably, over a dinner they had before shooting began, the hard-as-nails Crawford and the nail-biting Steven struck up a rapport. They would need every ounce of the good feeling generated. She was anxious off the set. She may also have had qualms about the potholes in the plot: a blind Park Avenue dowager blackmails a doctor and contrives to buy the eyes of a desperate gambler for a transplant. After rhapsodizing at length about her desire to see the sky, the birds, and so on, she unveils her new eyes not in daytime but at night, and on the night—no less—of the New York blackout. Never mind. Crawford's ferocious persona overrides questions of plausibility and carries its own conviction. Orange-haired and dagger-eyed, she was no less terrifying for being unseeing. Within the confines of limited space, Spielberg shows resourcefulness in composing scenes, keeping dialogue and monologues kinetic and watchable. He was a wreck when it was over, singed from his trial by fire. He learned a lot about making movies and about himself, possibly including a reluctance to use divas—or, at any rate, as he told Andy Warhol, those stars who bring their own baggage from film to film.

There were occasional assignments, but more often Spielberg was in limbo. He'd come upon a newspaper article about a Texas couple on the run who kidnap a cop in a desperate drive

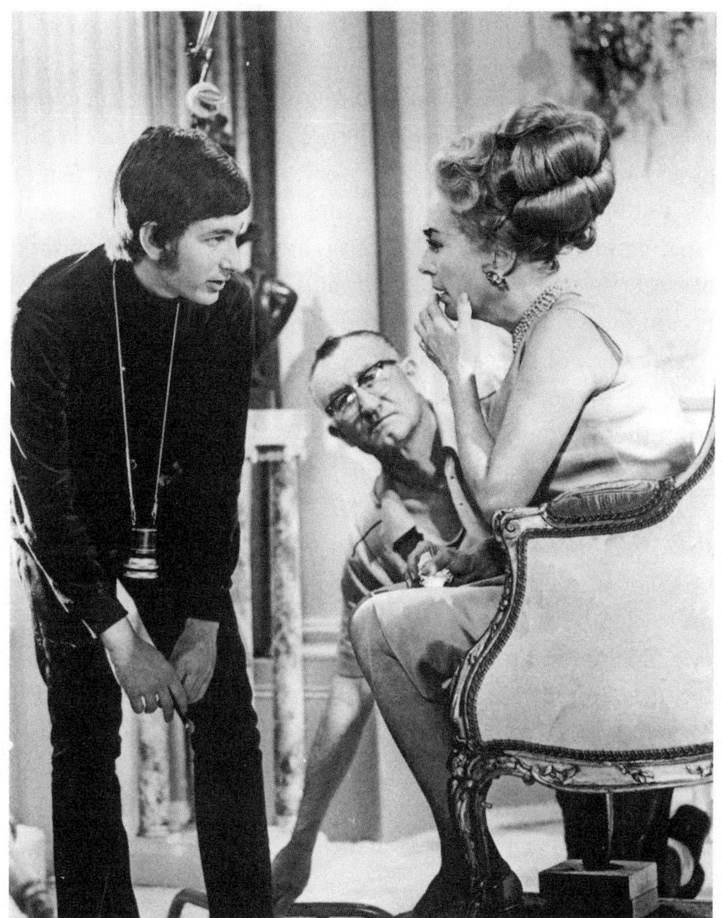

Diva and neophyte: Spielberg, twenty-two, and Joan Crawford, sixty-four, making an episode of *Night Gallery*. Universal TV/Photofest

to get their child from a foster home, but the studio rejected his idea for *The Sugarland Express* as too downbeat. After a hiatus, he came back to episodic television. He promised to be a good boy—no fancy angles, no time or footage overrun—yet he held his own in fights with the brass, and managed to find a way of adhering to the exigencies of television while exploiting his talent for giving a formulaic scene tension and visual energy. He could be proud of his work on *Marcus Welby, M.D.*; the first *Columbo* episode to air; and a futuristic segment of *The Name of the Game*, "LA 2017," became something of a classic. In the ninety-minute-long dystopian story, survivors of Los Angeles' unbreathable air have gone underground and organized a "shareholders democracy," which is anything but. The episode has echoes of *War of the Worlds* and anticipates later science fiction films that trade in the apocalyptic theme of a eugenics-based policy of selective survival. The series was itself an early display of a new seriousness regarding the genre, as it moved from the precincts of schlock to the status-y neighborhood of the high-gloss mass-appeal films of Spielberg and Lucas.

"Eulogy for a Wide Receiver," an episode of *Owen Marshall, Counselor at Law,* also looks prescient, dealing with the now hot theme of athletes on steroids. Arthur Hill was deeply impressed both by Spielberg's direction of actors and by his eye. "He seemed to be able to see more than other people saw." If Steven felt hamstrung by television's cookie-cutter approach to narrative, he admitted he'd learned how "to plan to do my homework every day" and not to waste time.[5]

Another of his efforts that won praise was an episode of *The Psychiatrist*, "Par for the Course" (1971), about a professional golfer (Clu Gulager) dying of cancer, with Joan Darling as his wife. Chuck Silvers was struck by how moving the episode was and wondered how the twenty-four-year-old understood such adult feelings. Steven told someone that he'd learned firsthand about age and illness from watching Grandpa Fievel in a nursing home, when the Posners lived near the Spielbergs in Arizona.

Joan Darling, who would later become one of the first women to direct television programs (for example, the wonderful *Mary Hartman, Mary Hartman*), was impressed with the young man's talent. She also noted that he was catching up in the social skills department, deftly negotiating parties as a careerist intent on meeting the right people.

Then came *Duel.* Although released in 1971 as a television movie, this terrifying and utterly original stalker film, in which a gigantic tanker truck relentlessly pursues a car over miles and miles of barren California highway, was unlike anything that was being done on the small screen. And a classic it is. Adapted from a Playboy story by Richard Matheson, the movie is an extended sick joke, virtually without dialogue, in which a hapless Dennis Weaver is at the wheel of the beleaguered car, while the truck driver looms unseen. The film is short (seventy-four minutes for TV, eighty-nine in its extended theatrical cut), but it works at such a pitch of terror that it would be unbearable if any longer.

The inspiration for Matheson, veteran writer for *The Twilight Zone*, came from an incident when, seven years earlier, he had been driving back to Los Angeles after playing golf when he heard the news of the Kennedy assassination. During the long ride from a round of golf with his partner, he became more and more enraged at a truck tailgating them, displacing his shock and outrage over the tragedy onto the bully at his back. Various executives in film and television had passed on the story, finding it too slight for a television episode, much less a feature film, but Steven immediately seized on it, and Barry Diller thought it could work as a movie of the week.

Matheson's fury paired with Spielberg's phobias proved an electric combination. The truck (for which Spielberg conducted a weeks-long casting search) is an overwhelmingly malefic presence, Weaver's driver a poor sap at the mercy of implacable forces of evil. Of course Steven would be attracted to this pearl of a story; what was not so inevitable was that he would turn it into such a mesmerizing little classic. Grouping it later with his subsequent films *The Sugarland Express* and *Jaws*, and always conscious of his not-yet-fixed place in the spectrum between commercial and serious, he would say that now he planned to do something besides cars, trucks, and sharks, as if he'd been playing with toys. Far from it.

Spielberg arrived in California a product of suburbia, with no thruway driving under his belt and a secondhand car that did little to steady his nerves. If it does nothing else, *Duel* speaks to all those phobics for whom getting behind the wheel is not the great all-American joy and the San Diego Freeway is a vehicular nightmare. But it does more. *Duel* has epic reach because Spielberg is instinctively broadening the definition of science fiction. The parable of the ordinary man, dwarfed by unknown forces, attains a kind of modest perfection here. He doesn't yet exhibit signs of grandiosity—the overreach and underlining—that are his besetting sins in the blockbusters to come.

What makes the movie so breathtaking is the way the terrors are held in a kind of equilibrium by Spielberg's extraordinary technical mastery. The hard-won lessons from television—how to avoid monotony and vary interest visually—pay off with interest. Moreover, he's still working in silent film: the duel to the death of car and truck requires neither dialogue nor the sort of characterization at which Spielberg is deficient—indeed, at one point he inserted, and later regretted, a kind of back story about Weaver's henpecked marriage, a harridan wife nagging Weaver over the telephone, and intimations of her infidelity.

The end is shattering; the sense of male impotence lingers disturbingly beyond the truck's "death." Spielberg would rarely conclude a film with such despair, although his next film, *The Sugarland Express*, comes close.

For the moment, he was riding high on the reception of *Duel*, which earned accolades for both the film and director. When Barry Diller saw a rough cut, he was both elated and saddened: elated because it was so good, and saddened because he realized instantly that Spielberg was too good for television, and he knew he'd never work with him again.

In Europe, where *Duel* was released as a feature film, it was a critical and commercial triumph. Critic Dilys Powell of *The Sunday Times* of London and David Lean both raved about the director's manipulations of space and the fluid sensuality and pleasure of his action scenes.[6] Spielberg also encountered the first of the Marxist adversaries who would constitute an opposition chorus attacking his films either at press conferences or in academic journals. After a showing of *Duel* in Italy, journalists walked out of the conference when he wouldn't agree on a left-wing political interpretation of the film, that *Duel* represented the "two Americas" or man versus "the system."

The Sugarland Express, Spielberg's first official feature-length theatrical movie, was another epic on wheels, an extravagantly choreographed police chase through the flatlands of Texas. Based on a newspaper account, it tells the story of a couple, both recently incarcerated, determined to wrest their baby from its foster home. After Lou Jean (Goldie Hawn), a beautician, has sexually blackmailed Clovis, her weak-willed husband (William Atherton) into escaping prison and accompanying her, they seize a state trooper (Michael Sacks) and, holding him hostage with his own gun, force him to drive them across the state of Texas with a cavalcade of state police in pursuit, becoming "family-values" folk heroes on the way. But Lou Jean the beautician, as conceived by Spielberg and played by an uncharacteristically tough and brassy Hawn, is no advertisement for Mother's Day. Instead, she's a sociopath version of "the little girl who never grew out of her pinafore."[7]

Spielberg, now in a rare mom-blaming period, has given the story his own matricidal spin. In the newspaper report on which the movie is based, it was the husband who plotted the kidnapping, and the wife was barely mentioned. Now it's the mother who's the driving force. In a shocking denouement, this woman who's incapable of empathy or insight sends her husband to his death, and it is the cops who mourn.

Critics noted the theme of deranged motherhood, and the strain of misogyny it revealed. "Misogyny" may be the wrong word, too broad and all-encompassing. One rarely feels hatred of women in Spielberg, but rather different shades of fear and mistrust. At this stage, if you exaggerated Leah's permissiveness and collusion, you might very well get an out-of-control mother whose love for her baby has nothing of the maternal in it.

"Walt Disney was my parental conscience," Spielberg told an interviewer, a loaded remark if there ever was one, since parents are notably absent, lost, and killed in Disney cartoons.[8] But the emotional and moral lesson of Disney is that parents may be missing in action, but they are never "bad," and the union of mother and child is a thing absolutely to be desired. *Sugarland*'s protagonist is a woman so unfit for motherhood that when we find out, courtesy of an afterword, that Lou Jean convinced the child welfare board that she was ready to care for little Langston and got him back, we feel appalled rather than relieved.

The first unorthodox move was to cast Goldie Hawn, lovable ditz, as a shrieking harridan. Spielberg needed a star, and to her credit, Goldie Hawn wanted the part. Her giggly, blond succulence is on display, but audiences expecting the tattooed, bikini-wearing bimbo of *Laugh-In* or the equally ingenuous, scantily clad madcap of *Butterflies Are Free* were in for a shock. Goldie Hawn's Lou Jean is abrasive and shrill, the first, but not the last, of that Spielberg archetype, the Shrieking Woman.

Nor does *Sugarland* have the romantic aura of most runaway couples movies, from *It Happened One Night* to *Bonnie and Clyde*, whereby a man and a woman are transformed by their odyssey. This odyssey transforms no one, and its vision of crowd madness and greed is closer to Billy Wilder's merciless *Ace in the Hole* than to the lyrical folksiness of *Badlands.* (With the police standing by helpless, the movie also raises the prophetic specter of an America whose might is at the mercy of fanatic individuals.)

With its carny atmosphere and tragic undertones, the movie shifts emotional gears moment by moment, and at the end we are left in some unresolved state between sadness and exasperation. There's a tonal complexity (some would say uncertainty) that would be unusual in the ultrapolished films to come. For the most part, critics were positive, but predictably, it was not a popular success; hence, to the director who sought popularity over esteem, it was a failure, and a mistake he vowed he would never make again. By mistake, he presumably meant all the things that make it compelling—the mixing of tones, the Vietnam-era pessimism, and above all, the unsympathetic portrayal of the two main characters.

The only reason we don't despise the couple completely is that there are characters with moral authority who love or pity them and see some possibility of redemption hidden to most of us. "They're just kids," says Ben Johnson as a police captain, and the kidnapped cop who has a Stockholm syndrome crush on his kidnappers, tries to reason with them.

"A lot of Steven went into this film," said Vilmos Zsigmond, his brilliant cinematographer, who felt he was "never better."

He drew on exceptional talents: in addition to Zsigmond, he benefited from a sharp screenplay by Hal Barwood and Matthew Robbins (with his own credited contributions), and a first score by John Williams, with whom he would work happily throughout his career.

The movie is a showcase of dazzling camera moves, dollies, impossible tracking shots, the camera hanging like a trapeze artist inside the car, the *corps de flics* snaking through the flatlands of Texas. But he also shows his genius for never letting the pyrotechnics overwhelm human drama. People on the set were astounded by his command of the language of filmmaking, comparing him with none other than Orson Welles. Producer Richard Zanuck watched him on the first day of shooting and said he didn't think he'd ever worked with anyone who knew the mechanics of moviemaking as well as Steven. The art and production directors were equally stunned, as was Zsigmond. The cinematographer who had worked with Robert Altman on *McCabe and Mrs. Miller* and *The Long Goodbye* said that Spielberg was a joy to work with. He didn't yet know everything—but he soon would. So he asked questions and was always willing to try something new. There was a great deal of give and take: he and Zsigmond watched lots of films; he wanted something "grittier and less self-consciously stylized" than the Altman movies, and he wanted European (natural) lighting to give it a documentary feeling.[9]

Pauline Kael, who wanted cinema to thrill and excite her, was particularly attuned to Spielberg's perpetual motion machine, and wrote a prescient review of *The Sugarland Express.* "He could be that rarity among directors—a born entertainer. . . . In terms of the pleasure that technical assurance gives an audience, this film is one of the most phenomenal debut films in the history of movies. If there is such a thing as movie sense . . . Spielberg really has it. But he may be so full of it that he doesn't have much else."[10]

The "much else" would come: edifying stories, "big" themes, but the movies that boasted such claims to importance weren't inherently better because of it.

His exceptional affinity with children is revealed in one delicate, offhand scene when Baby Langdon (played by Zanuck's son Harrison) is on the lawn, cavorting with his dog, and tries to get him to eat by miming it the way his foster mother has done with him. This spontaneous gesture also tells you all you need to know about the warmth and security of his foster parents, the only image of a functioning family.

There's one moment in the film where our feelings for the couple deepen into something like sympathy and a foreshadowing of loss. Lou Jean and Clovis are sitting in the car at night, watching a Road Runner cartoon playing at a nearby drive-in. As there is no sound, Clovis is making up dialogue, and Lou Jean is laughing hysterically. It is a brief moment of unalloyed joy, perhaps the only one, and it ends abruptly when the bird, after hitting his head repeatedly against brick walls, leaps, falls splat, into a void, to rise no more. It's a brilliant and devastating touch: the normally resilient cartoon character meeting his apparent end.

For Spielberg, who grew up on them, cartoons are not just a reference point, something he uses for metaphor or analogy, but a crucial part of his artistic sensibility. To say his narratives are cartoonlike is descriptive rather than invidious. Their rhythms, their chase patterns, their frenzies, even their generic sense of unchanging character—these elements feature more obviously in his early films, but the later ones also owe a good deal to his days watching Disney, Looney Tunes, and the like. But those aspects of the cartoon on which their vitality and charm depend—the repetitiveness, the stubborn resistance to change—also work better in short form: time, as in a feature film, demands change, growth, nuance.

Spielberg was going to be very careful about what he did next. *Le succès d'estime* is all well and good for the fancy-pants European and American auteurs, but not for Cecil B. DeSpielberg. He sought waves of emotion, craved an audience whose excitement was as great as his own. The Boy Scout impresario wanted to recapture the explosion of laughs he'd had from his fellow Scouts at his first public film, the frissons of terror when he'd told them horror stories around the campfire. He was headed toward something that didn't yet exist, that he would help bring into being: the mass-marketed must-see summer film, the saturation booking at that new and suddenly ubiquitous institution, the multiplex.

But first there were early efforts to make *Close Encounters of the Third Kind*, a large-scale version of his 8 mm science fiction film *Firelight* that he'd been dying to make for more than ten years. He first approached Gloria Katz and Willard Huyck, the screenwriting couple who were at work on *American Graffiti*, but got a quick no. Science fiction—imagined as flying saucers and stick people—was still B movie material, regarded as trash by anyone with serious film aspirations. It didn't help Steven with Katz and Huyck that he had first gone to them with an even less appetizing idea: a film he wanted to direct—*Crapper*—about the inventor of the toilet.

Meanwhile, his schmoozing skills had improved. He was getting chummy with the beach crowd, specifically with Julia and Michael Phillips, who, coming off the success of *The Sting*, considered him the most talented of all the would-be auteurs at Nicholas Beach and were interested in producing his next movie. They were pitching this remake of his own *Firelight* to Columbia. But it was still amorphous, by Julia's own admission, "an idea in search of a movie."[11]

As discussions stumbled, something formidable emerged from the watery deep.

5

Jaws *"Open Wide"*

TAKING THEIR STRATEGIES from the playbook of Hitchcock, two of the scariest movies of the mid-1970s depend not on a supernatural enemy or a Frankenstein monster but on the moment when a familiar, everyday environment turns hostile, exposing humankind at its most vulnerable. A year after the ocean had become a crime scene in *Jaws*, the dentist's chair took its turn in *Marathon Man*, another film that also looks into the mandibles of death. Who can forget Laurence Olivier's fiendish Nazi slowly angling an electric probe toward Dustin Hoffman's mouth? People canceled their dentist appointments; they stopped going into the ocean.

Spielberg's adaptation of Peter Benchley's best-selling book, a hellish and difficult production from beginning to end, made up for the madness and the tsuris when it opened to acclaim and gradually hit the box office stratosphere, surpassing *The Godfather* as the highest-grossing film of all time. *Jaws* would also inaugurate the summer blockbuster and change the distribution pattern of movies, which would open wide, and then wider.

People did eventually go back to the dentist, but some never went back into the water. So powerful was the continual hold of *Jaws* that we couldn't think about real shark attacks without instantly, involuntarily, summoning up the images and sounds from the movie. In the early summer of 2015, just as America was gearing up for the film's fortieth anniversary rerelease, nature provided its own tie-in: two youngsters lost arms to sharks off the coast of North Carolina. Spielberg's 1975 thriller, already as unavoidable a staple of summer as heat and humidity, now became the reference point for the real-life horror, providing the money shot for footage that would have otherwise lacked visual excitement. Once again Spielberg had surpassed God in his mastery of mise-en-scène.

The problems of filming the story of a great white shark terrorizing a summer village (the Hamptons in the book; Martha's Vineyard in the movie) were not entirely unforeseeable: to the usual ones of budget, script, and casting (an actors strike was threatened) were added that of training a shark (yes, that was the original plan!), of shooting on Martha's Vineyard in high summer season, of the crew being cooped up on an island for months with little but bars and barmaids for entertainment. For all these reasons and more, most producers didn't want to touch *Jaws* with a barge pole. Like *Gone with the Wind*, one of its notable blockbuster predecessors, the novel was a best seller that could invite invidious comparisons, and like *GWTW* it was just too complicated, impossible to film, and impossible to cast—especially the star. In other words, how do you cast the central role of a man-eating monster? In the case of *Jaws*, do you go with a live or a mechanical great white? And do you go with a veteran action director or a neophyte whose David Selznickian reach and expertise had yet to be revealed?

Water safety: swimmers exit the water with all deliberate haste in *Jaws*.
Universal Pictures/Photofest

After first wanting, then deciding against, a reliable "engineer" of a director, producers Richard Zanuck and David Brown decided to take a risk and hire "the kid." Nor was the talented if less experienced director without qualms. He wanted to entertain, but he also wanted to be known as a serious filmmaker.

Other people hesitated and passed. Writers Richard Levinson and William Link, collaborators and supporters from his television days, not only declined to write the screenplay, they tried to persuade their friend to forget about the whole thing. Richard Dreyfuss, who wasn't the first actor approached to play the oceanographer Hooper, was nevertheless reluctant, since the scientist lost his life early in the original screenplay. In an amusing reversal of this pattern, Charlton Heston actively sought the role of the Ahab-like fisherman Quint, and Spielberg turned him down. He was wrong for the part; the savior of mankind would hardly be hanging out in a tiny little island community, but it was satisfying payback as well: Heston had declined the kid's overtures in the Universal canteen, and now he could spurn the veteran star.

Spielberg wisely eliminated the adulterous love affair of the book, and suggested class distinctions without belaboring them. After scripts were written and discarded, it was Carl Gottlieb, friend, writer, and sometime actor (he plays the newspaper man in the film), who ended up collaborating with Steven as the two worked with the actors—unusual for Spielberg—during the filming, making changes as they went along.

Two key decisions, both involving casting—Hooper and the shark—were almost happenstance. The first, which steered the film in a more personal direction, was Spielberg's opting to go with Dreyfuss. For the director he represented "the underdog in all of us." Moreover, he was a natural Spielberg stand-in: Jewish, smart, hyper, and a rapid-fire talker. Hooper was originally slated for an early descent into a watery grave, but the second-unit scene with his double went awry and the oceanographer was allowed to live another day, sharing protagonist duties with Roy Scheider's sheriff Brody. Another accident, another crucial shift: not only enriching the film but bringing it seamlessly in tune with a Darwinian shift in the Zeitgeist, an atmosphere favoring the rise and revenge of the nerd, brain over brawn.

As for the shark, the original idea was to capture the great white in its natural habitat, in the waters off Australia. But when two National Geographic cinematographers met with near-disaster, plan B went into effect, and a mechanical shark was made at the studio. The dummy—or rather, dummies (there were three of them), called Bruce after Spielberg's lawyer—proved nearly as intractable and unwieldy as the live shark. Realizing how hopeless and phony the mechanical shark was—Bruce, large or small, looked about as real as the Tin Man—Steven had to think outside of the box, and he found the kind of imaginative solution that an embryonic technology called computer-enhanced graphics would soon render obsolete. Emulating Hitchcock, the artist of indirection, he decided to show the mechanical shark as infrequently as possible. The camera would glide along at sea level, where the animal would always be suggested but rarely seen. The visual ellipsis created far greater menace and terror, as the shark is nowhere and everywhere. The cutting (Verna Fields was the terrific editor) and Spielberg's use of reverse zoom create a jittery atmosphere, underscored (in both senses) by John Williams's thrumming bass, eerily vibrating through the waters, its four-note motif the pulsating heart of the film. At any moment the stillness will be broken as the huge silver tumescence explodes through the surface, his razor teeth glinting in the sun.

Steven always insisted on one more take, one more effort to improve the shark, and while everybody else wanted to wrap and get out of there, the director was uncompromising. According to Gottlieb, "Most of the company never saw him sweat, . . . and no one but me would ever know what his doubts and anxieties were. There aren't many survivors of 'the Fish Movie,' but I think all of us would agree that Spielberg was precociously self-assured about his filmmaking, and rarely shared any feelings of self-doubt that he might be swimming in very deep waters, professionally speaking."

The crew members might have been impressed, but they were also boiling with resentment. Spielberg got wind of a plot to throw him overboard when the film finished shooting, so he laid out the shot and secretly skipped town in a speedboat. A getaway car was waiting, and on the long drive to Boston, he began twitching uncontrollably, in a jittery reaction to the sudden lights and sounds of the mainland. At his hotel that night, he had a full-scale anxiety attack, described by Gottlieb in *The*

Jaws Log as like an electric shock, "complete with sweaty palms, tachycardia, difficulty breathing, and vomiting."[1] Nightmares of Martha's Vineyard plagued him for months.

Hardly less visceral were audience reactions. A relentless "attack on the audiences' nerves," as one critic observed, had viewers vomiting, screaming, laughing, some rushing from the theater, most coming back, and then returning for another assault. Frank Rich at *New Times* was dazzled by Spielberg's storytelling talent, but not a few critics were resistant to its spell.[2] A "coldly efficient fright machine," demurred one. Vincent Canby of the *New York Times* saw it as a formulaic science fiction film in which a nightmare monster emerges from the deep.[3] "It's a noisy, busy movie that has less on its mind than any child at the beach," he wrote, echoing Pauline Kael's criticism that Spielberg's films weren't *about* anything. Other reviewers complained about its machinelike manipulation, among them the usually benign Charles Champlin of the *Los Angeles Times*, William Pechter in *Commentary*, and (as McBride reminds me) yours truly in the *Village Voice*, where I wrote that it made me feel "like a rat being given shock treatment."[4]

One of the film's recent defenders, Antonia Quirke, wrote in an elegant monograph that it was precisely this absence of deeper meaning or purpose on Spielberg's part that made the film so effective, as thrillingly graceful and kinetic as an Astaire-Rogers dance routine.[5] But this is a revisionist view, seeing the film in the context of what came after, and as avatar of something called "pure cinema." At the time, more critics noted a disturbing sign of regression in the film's appeal to an escalating hunger for physical thrills and instant gratification.

Were the fears mostly male, or was *Jaws* tapping into a general fearfulness concerning the uncertainties of the future, the paranoia endemic to post-sixties America? The portrait of the mayor as willing to risk lives to keep the cushy little frolic of a resort open for the Fourth of July reflects the general mistrust in our leaders and institutions that was just beginning its wholesale slide into cynicism. A "conduit," as one critic said of American films of the period, "for the shudder that went through the culture"?[6] Or, as *Newsweek* suggested, "primal fears buried deep in the collective unconscious of all mankind."[7]

It was open season for Freudian sleuths. There was the threat posed by the women's movement, now amassing on the horizon. The shark was not only the tumescent penis, it was the razor-edge *vagina dentata* of the female's entry site. Like woman, the shark is threatening because she is shadowy and ubiquitous, everywhere and nowhere. The threat had to be countered by not one, or two, but three stalwarts of the stronger sex.

Spielberg was at least partly in on the joke. The three male leads represented three versions of insecurity. Robert Shaw's Captain Quint, a parody of the high school superjock, is a swaggering penis competing with Superdick-shark. He's also the sort of hero that Spielberg, unlike many of his peers, will never present with a totally straight face. Dreyfuss is the hippieish Jewish intellectual, the problem solver nerd, while Scheider's Sheriff Brody, a transplanted New Yorker who's afraid of boats and water, is nevertheless a responsible Family Man. In one hilariously puerile male bonding scene, Dreyfuss's jock envy comes to the fore as he and Shaw slug back apricot brandy, comparing scars and hard-life stories.

Lurking beneath their Robert Bly men-around-the-campfire moment is that deeper and more generalized adolescent dread—of the Female in her many guises, starting with the girl who's always a little more grown up than the boys her age and who, in classic horror-film setup, is the first to go, thus displacing the blame for male desires onto the "insatiable" woman.

Blond, tipsy Chrissie—yes, she actually has a name—is the shark's first victim in *Jaws*' iconic opening scene, the girl who breaks away from the beach party and races to the water, lithely stripping as she goes along, while the poor graceless guy stumbles over his feet trying to climb out of his pants. Susan Backlinie, the actress and stuntwoman who, in a Spielberg in-joke, would also play shark bait in *1941*, may be the only sexy babe in all of his films. And look what happens to her!

There's a further satisfaction of sorts in unleashing the monster on that other monster, the Shrieking Woman. No wonder we're more frightened for the dog. SHUT UP! we want to yell, but the shark performs the service in our stead, and with so little fuss. Hence a certain sneaky sympathy for the beast; compared to all these meatheads around him, the fish, in fine King Kong tradition, is just doing what his/her species does, quietly and with dignity.

Afterward, when reviewers attacked the film's manipulative violence, Spielberg offered words of penance. He had, he acknowledged, made a "primal scream . . . raw nerve movie," and could have "made a very subtle movie if I'd wanted to."[8] Since such a film is hard to imagine, if not self-contradictory, this must be taken as Spielberg, always aware of his image, in spinmeister mode. Every moment was calculated. He had noted the absence of a second-act climax, and so created one—a head coming out of the hole in the boat—shot in Verna Fields's swimming pool.

Its huge success and its thriller nature worked against *Jaws* at Oscar time. Spielberg expected it to be nominated in eleven categories, including Best Director. On the day the nominations were announced, he even had a television crew in his office, to record what he expected would be a triumphant run. He was crushed when he failed to make the Best Director cut. Nevertheless, *Jaws* had its revenge, not only at the box office, but as a giant step in a moviemaking and marketing revolution.

Instead of a prestige picture opening on a few select urban screens, then slowly going "wide" to smaller cities and second-run theaters, the summer blockbuster would be an event, with ubiquitous advertising creating the aura of a "must-see" film. Eventually *Jaws* opened on more than four hundred screens in the chains of multiplexes that had sprouted up across the country. There would be tie-ins: reissues of the book, T-shirts, spin-off products.

Over time, the term "blockbuster" itself would change, no longer referring to an actual hit, a movie the public has embraced, but to a business model or "product," at the conceptual stage rather than at its consummation, and based, preferably and almost invariably, on a pretested "property"—the comic book franchise, the superhero thriller, the action adventure.

The other element of huge significance was the Youth Audience. In an article on seventies films in *Film Comment,* Richard Corliss cited a Motion Picture Association of America survey that found that forty-nine percent of all moviegoers were between the ages of twelve and twenty, and another twenty-seven percent were between twenty-one and twenty-nine.[9] And, unmentioned, was that many of these young people were male, and many would go to see the film again and again—the much-coveted "repeater" audience. After all, as Morris Dickstein points out, Disney had long profited by tying in movies with TV series, comic books, theme parks, and toys (like Davy Crockett's coonskin cap). But for Disney "the culture of childhood was still a separate realm of wishful fantasy, a never-never-land of the kind J. M. Barrie had conjured up in Peter Pan."[10]

The Hollywood honchos were thrilled with the kind of success that *Jaws* and *Close Encounters* represented, thanks to which they would soon become even more supremely rich (and insecure). They had tapped into an audience that was vaster and far more reliable than the hippies and the pointy heads and the buffs who made *Easy Rider* and *Midnight Cowboy* successful. Or even the middlebrow audiences who had made hits of *The Towering Inferno, Earthquake,* and *Airport 1975* but were increasingly staying home. Youth. Real youth was not counterculture-with-facial-hair youth but Teenagers.

The irony is that *Jaws*, the assault on the jugular, begins to look like a humanist gem in comparison with the assembly-line franchises that followed, thanks partly to the magnetism of family. The sympathetic mother, the urban cop who's out of his depth, the boy who mimics his father: these may not be full-fledged characterizations, but they represent something human, warm and inviting, a sanctuary that holds its own even against the charisma of the shark.

What Peter Biskind hailed, in *Easy Riders, Raging Bulls: How the Sex-Drugs-and-Rock-'n'-Roll Generation Saved Hollywood*, as a period of glory and experiment, with the work of democratizing filmmakers replacing sclerotic studio entertainment, lasted barely a decade.

This golden age, though, was part mirage, part myth, part fluke and aberration, and was hardly a blueprint for any conceivable golden future. The favored talents of the New Cinema were the exception rather than the rule. The idea that the "movie brats" exercised real power to make personal films, David Puttnam suggests, was a "seductive myth created by the media. . . . Their real strength was an ability and willingness to work with the system, even if it meant sacrificing some aspects of their personal vision."[11]

The brief for the defense was critic Tom Shone. In his 2004 book *Blockbuster*, he would mount a spirited broadside, championing Spielberg and Lucas, crediting them with reinvigorating Hollywood, as against Peter Biskind's morose view of the triumph of trash over art in the early seventies. With curled lip and a younger generation's respect for box-office clout, Shone portrays Biskind and his ilk as losers in the record books of film history: we've sat through the impenetrable *longueurs* of Ukrainian cinema, the scraping tedium of Cassavetes, and the churning angst of Scorsese only to discover that we've backed the wrong horse. We've missed the point that Spielberg is "the most talented filmmaker of his generation" because he's simply too successful, and because he does it all so effortlessly.[12]

There's some truth in this, but what Shone doesn't acknowledge is the coarsening of taste and expectations in the wake (and imitation) of those early blockbusters, and the audiences they cultivated. When he defends his youthful enthusiasm against us killjoys, what is he defending?

The Peter Pan "in all of us"; an elevation of nostalgia to first principle. Shone's paean to the blockbuster is a valorization not of his adult, cinephile, art-film-plus passions but of his fourteen-year-old first loves. He sees the excitement generated by *Star Wars* or *Close Encounters* or *Jaws* not as something one is meant to outgrow, but as a permanent gold standard of taste, of feelings too precious to be left behind. For baby boomers, and their successors of Generations X, Y, and Z, nostalgia had itself become big business, with ever-shortening time lapses, and each decade's childhood favorites returning to console in a kind of endless spin cycle.

Asked about its success, Spielberg at one point said he felt *Jaws* made it safe to express fear in public without "the macho cover."

Or did it make it safe for men—as in his other films—to regress into their adolescent selves where the fears are real, even primal, but not particularly complex? In a 2011 interview, Spielberg would confess to his lifelong anxiety and nail-biting. "Yes, I've always had shpilkes. I have it now. I had it then. It is my fuel, basically."[13] He perhaps understood that phobias, like fetishes, are containers that keep even greater terrors at bay, like the adult anxieties that permeate and haunt a Hitchcock film: Ambivalence, desire, shame, morbidity, self-delusion, Oedipal longings, and inexpiable guilt, these are the subliminal monsters reflected in but not restricted to the "scare" scenes, and for which there is no harpoon, or safe landing.

6

Close Encounters of the Third Kind

We're so accustomed to seeing Spielberg through the prism of success, a magician who can do no wrong, that it's easy to forget what risky propositions *Jaws* and *Close Encounters of the Third Kind* were at the time.

The actual genesis of *Close Encounters* was a short story Steven wrote in 1970. "Experiences" was set in a small midwestern town; a boy and a girl are parked on "lovers' lane" when they're startled by a light show in the sky. This conjunction of hormonal teenagers and otherworldly retribution was a common horror-film setup. In 1957's *The Blob*, for example, a young Steve McQueen and his pretty date are on a mountaintop when the eponymous invader appears like a shooting star. This motif formed the premise of Spielberg's earlier *Firelight*, but by *Close Encounters*, horny teenagers would be safely shrunk into a G-rated kid—a kid who can feel innocent wonder, unmixed with adult (that is, sexual) guilt.

UFOs were the bogeymen of science films of the fifties and sixties, low-budget B movies that were rarely reviewed and were never in contention for awards. This was part of their charm. Their tacky, under-the-radar quality allowed for a kind of "termite art" that movie buffs would miss after Spielberg burnished the genre to a high gloss. But in planning *Close Encounters* as a big-budget film, Spielberg intended that the UFOs would be taken very seriously. Possibly because he himself took them seriously. If he wasn't an all-out True Believer, he wasn't a nonbeliever either.

The story, after various rewrites, would be a switch on the Cold War paranoia of those movies Spielberg had grown up on, such as *The Thing*, *Invasion of the Body Snatchers*, and his own *Firelight*. With their apocalyptic scenarios of deadly aliens planning a nuclear Armageddon, these B movies fed on what Susan Sontag called the "imagination of disaster," and had predictable alignments—sacredness of family and the American way of life, the good-guy hero at one end; somewhere in the middle (he could go either way), the mad scientist; and the insidious, ingenious enemy; and despite low budgets, sufficient resources to create spectacular disaster footage, suggesting the seductive allure of mass destruction.[1]

Spielberg would upend these traditional fifties alignments, as well as the doom-laden scenarios fashionable in the seventies, a decade of national malaise, furious discord, failing cities, Watergate hearings, and politically loaded films. Drawing from the benign-alien tradition of *The Day the Earth Stood Still* and Stanley Kubrick's *2001* (as well as science fiction writers like Arthur C. Clarke, on whose short story "The Sentinel" *2001* is based), Spielberg's new aliens may cause a bit of disruption, but they are not out to destroy the earth; rather, they are ambassadors of peace, all too happy to take their best earth friends aboard when they depart.

The project was both counterintuitive and uncategorizable. Science fiction films weren't "in." And it wasn't quite a science fiction film, was it? It was as much family melodrama as thriller. And as much a metaphysical quest and cosmic sound-and-light show as either.

Why was Julia Phillips interested in this weird project that struck the screenwriting Huycks as a nonstarter? Possibly an even more interesting subplot would be why David Begelman bit. But then, the ex-agent turned producer, whose financial turpitudes would be juicily documented in David McClintick's best-selling biography *Indecent Exposure*, was known even by himself as a wild man and self-saboteur, a "Prince of Darkness."[2] He had a string of successes, a Hollywood asset for which many questionable activities could be overlooked. But the studio he headed was failing, and he was about to be exposed as a liar, embezzler, and forger. He couldn't know that he and Columbia Pictures, their fates intertwined, would be saved by of the success of this oddball film for which Julia Phillips was desperately trying get a green light. Begelman would be spared an indictment, and his crimes would be covered up—a pattern that would persist through many more felonies and schemes from the Ponzi playbook—until, sinking into major debt, his victims closing in, he shot himself in a hotel room in 1995.

Perhaps he simply wanted to be in on the "youth" market. There was a prior connection with Spielberg, whose agent he had been before going to Columbia. He was also the sort of front-office scoundrel to whom Steven was often attracted. Or maybe Begelman felt a kindred spirit in Phillips, who was a loose cannon of a different, newer kind. She did have an Academy Award for an old-style hit under her belt. But she was also, as she herself admitted, a drug-addled depressive mess, flying off in all directions. She was producing *Taxi Driver* as well as a baby, was getting divorced, and had optioned Erica Jong's *Fear of Flying* for the simple reason that she herself was terrified of flying, and wanted to direct.

She was taking meetings with "DB," trying to figure out how to describe the film, circling the room with almost nothing concrete to offer, but shooting off ideas in bursts of sparks. The pitch: "Anyone who has dropped acid and looked up at the sky for a while or smoked a joint and watched the Watergate hearings on TV is waiting for this movie. And it is uniquely this group of people who is going to give it to them. Hubris and youth and the promise of really good drugs fire these ambitions."[3]

If her prophecy had proved correct, the audiences would have filled only a few small theaters. Yet she was onto something, touching on the hip side of a film that would have crossover appeal, plugging into both the family audiences and the counterculture, a group to which Steven didn't actually belong because he didn't do drugs. He was the boy with ambition in his heart and a necktie in his guitar case. But he also was someone who didn't need to do drugs. He could simply "look at the sky for a while"—the meteor shower he'd witnessed back in Arizona with his father—and get high. The sense of wonder was inborn and uncrushable.

It was as close as you come to a religious feeling. We live in a secular age in which artists wrestle with nihilism, and any expression of faith is both rare and unfashionable. Even those directors who grew up under the influence, like the lapsed Catholics Altman, Coppola, Scorsese, have a tortured relationship with their church, while Spielberg seems to have been born with a religious sense of awe the way others are born short or gregarious or curly-haired. He bows not to God or orthodoxy, but to the otherworldly and the ineffable. Mel Gibson or Scorsese or Pasolini may make a film about Christ, but *Close Encounters* makes us feel the power of a religious calling, a vocation summoning one out of the blue in a leap of faith leaving all behind.

A Hollywood film with religious conviction: how was this

possible? For the simple reason that Steven, the boy who'd heard voices speaking to him on the radio, who'd swallowed a transistor, who thought his fillings contained messages, who'd felt knocked out of his body by the Ark of the Torah, who'd watched shooting stars with his father in Arizona, who'd followed Rod Serling (who'd followed André Breton and the Surrealists) into the fifth dimension, this Steven believed in the possibility of life elsewhere, messengers from another zone.

Before the script took its final shape, there were a number of efforts, action-thriller screenplays and those—or one, at least—of a more metaphysical bent: "Kingdom Come" by Paul Schrader. Schrader, the ex-Calvinist who had started as a film critic, was now embarking on a filmmaking career.

That Spielberg and Schrader were on different wavelengths soon became clear, as Schrader reports in *Schrader on Schrader.* His script was about a modern-day St. Paul who starts as a debunker and turns into a believer, eventually finding the light of the universe within himself.

Little of his script was left in the movie. "What I had done was to write this character with resonances of Lear and St. Paul, a kind of Shakespearean tragic hero, and Steve just could not get behind that, and it became clear that our collaboration had to end. It came down to this. I said, 'I refuse to send the guy off to start a McDonald's franchise.' Steven said he wanted an ordinary man, precisely the sort who would want to set up a McDonald's franchise on another planet. Steven's Capra-like infatuation with the common man was diametrically opposed to my religious infatuation with the redeeming hero."[4]

Yet the Roy Neary who answers The Call doesn't come close to being the sort of guy to plant a McDonald's arch in outer space.

A child's sense of wonder Steven Spielberg might have, but that didn't mean he was lacking in practicality. A shrewd negotiator, he stunned the Phillipses by calculating precisely the highest figure he could propose to Begelman and have him accept. (This was before *Jaws;* the amount, which the producer agreed to, was an unheard of $2.7 million.) In the event, *Close Encounters* proved more technically difficult than *Jaws,* and would climb by stages, first to $11.5 million, then to a final cost of $22 million, eventually requiring a studio and sound stage created out of a giant dirigible hangar in Mobile, Alabama. And then Spielberg wanted to blend fantasy and reality in unusual ways, but knew nothing about the necessary optical effects, which turned out to be incredibly complicated, and whose outcome couldn't be determined until a finished print.

Spielberg would claim sole writing credit, even though he cited five screenwriters who helped at various points, and there were reportedly many sub-rosa rewrites. Spielberg acknowledged that Hal Barwood and Matthew Robbins had worked on the story (each also had a small part in the film); John Hill worked on a draft, and David Giler and Jerry Belson helped polish the script.

The apportionment of credit, particularly in scriptwriting, would be a hot-button issue throughout Spielberg's career, with charges of inadequate attribution in the wake of a number of his films, and, in his use of existing work and historical subjects, charges of plagiarism or copyright violation. Such arguments are legion in Hollywood—after all, that's what the lawyers for the Screenwriters Guild are paid handsome sums to adjudicate. But success, as they say, has many fathers: it's rare that anyone disputes credits for a failed movie, and Spielberg's movies were plagued by paternity claims, if not suits.

Although he *could* write, he hated it because of the huge amount of concentration required; his mind was always firing off in too many directions. "Essentially I'm not a writer and I don't enjoy writing. I'd much rather collaborate. I need fresh ideas coming to me."[5]

One problem is that we know what's *in* a film—in this case De Palma supposedly suggested the shape of the "mountain," and Michael Phillips pushed to have the aliens benign. But we don't know what got left out, which ideas were rejected out of hand, which were tried and dismissed, or which floated along some obscure nonscripted route into the finished film. He absorbed influences—old movies, friends' suggestions—as part of his daily diet, but was, as was increasingly clear, very much his own man, his self-disparagements (or feints) about not having a directorial personality or "signature" style notwithstanding.

His films would always be a blender of high and low influences, from the cheesiest television serials to the sublime imagery of John Ford. Past and present would intermingle, with memories from the storehouse of childhood viewing as vivid to the adult Spielberg as those he borrowed and reworked from movies he screened each night after a day of shooting. Disney's influence on *Close Encounters* emerged in the theme song—"When You Wish upon a Star," the Jiminy Cricket song from *Pinocchio*—and on a spookier level, the amazing "Night on Bald Mountain" sequence from *Fantasia*, that extended *danse macabre* in which a demon raises spirits of the dead—bat-winged monsters, skeletal horses and riders, skulls and hellfires leaping to the music of Mussorgsky.

The site chosen was Devil's Tower National Monument, near Gillette, Wyoming, which bears an obvious association with Monument Valley, the western landscape used by John Ford, the great American director whose DNA can be found in almost every young director of this time.

You could say that artists naturally gravitate to those whom they know or sense will give them what they need in terms of ideas and advice. If Spielberg was influenced, it was in a direction in which he was already headed. He resisted obvious plot lines that were trendy or politically fashionable—for example, the highly topical theme of government cover-up—a difference that separated him from Schrader and many of his contemporaries. Though the usual blustering bureaucrats and civil service functionaries do appear, hinting at cover-ups, Spielberg, according to Schrader, decided not to do the film as a UFO Watergate.

By refusing to get bogged down in the political theme, Spielberg keeps his emphasis (as in *Jaws*) on the unorthodox, on characters who are intellectually curious, willing to go halfway: the scientist played by François Truffaut, his interpreter, played by Bob Balaban, and the people who hang out each night on the country road, waiting, watching. The director isn't interested in a Manichaean face-off between good and evil, or even nasty federal bureaucrats. *His* people are the UFO believers who line the roadside at night and protest government actions. A more skeptical viewer might see this rag-tag group of misfits and loners as potential ISIS recruits, malcontents ripe for a cause, but to Spielberg they constitute a benign brotherhood of nonconformists like Roy, childlike in their yearning to believe in something "larger" than themselves.

Douglas Turnbull, who'd been visual effects supervisor on *2001*, was designing the extraterrestrials, a risk that Kubrick had avoided by simply never showing them. Kubrick feared that people would laugh at the cliché of spindly figures with oversize heads. I confess to siding with Kubrick on this one. I find the aliens creepy, and the finale wildly overblown. Spielberg is brilliant with crowds, but here the effect is slightly repellent, grandiose, the sacred visitors encased in a nimbus of light, suggestive of a celestial super-rally, a Triumph of the Willies. Still, most spectators are as spellbound as Spielberg himself is, thanks to the filmmaker's emotional investment in the extraterrestrials with a sincerity Kubrick never could have managed.

By contrast, it is the family itself, usually so sacrosanct, that is jarringly grim. Roy Neary lives in a domestic hell. He is the Peter Pan in the family, more youthful in spirit than his children: he wants to go and see *Pinocchio*, and tries to engage his surly older son in a session with electric trains. The latter is sullen with boredom, while the younger son, jealous of his baby sister, smashes a doll against the crib while issuing blood-curdling screams, breaking both its little legs (as Steven had decapitated his sisters' dolls). The mother, played by Teri Garr, is scoldy and querulous, ignores the ruckus and dismemberment, and (the kiss of death) refuses to listen to any discussion of the UFO emergency. If this is the New Hollywood, it is no place for actresses. The normally attractive Garr is cruelly deglamorized and subjected to humiliating rejection when later she tries to reignite the couple's romantic fires at the most inopportune moment: during the midnight vigil on the highway, while everyone's watching the sky expectantly, waiting for the UFO. The message is clear: girls, don't mess with your guys when they're playing with their toys. As it happens, at this very time, while filming in Texas, Spielberg had met and become involved with a woman, who would return with him to California. Eventually she would leave him for reasons of incompatibility—she couldn't share his enthusiasm for films.

Suburbia is no refuge, no community of congenial souls in a little nest, insulated from the world. In this hostile environment Roy becomes increasingly possessed by the idea of the alternate reality embodied in the spaceship whose shape is lodged in his mind, and which he is compelled to re-create. The home and family have become so toxic that a deranged Neary must literally uproot it, ploughing up the lawn, pouring dirt into the house to recast the huge mound that calls to him from outer space.

Spielberg had wanted Jack Nicholson for the part, but when Nicholson was unavailable he went with Dreyfuss, and once again a movie of his took a more personal turn. Like his character in *Jaws*, Dreyfuss is the truth seeker, but even before he leaves his family, he seems out of his element in white-bread America, an alien cut off from his tribe.

Roy is hard to get close to, an enigma that has to do with his "calling," but also perhaps with Spielberg's confusion about his identity at this stage in his life. In one sense he represents an all-American type, Leslie Fiedler's mythic archetype of the wandering man, the refugee from domesticity. But Dreyfuss's Roy Neary is a complex, even confusing, composite of family dynamics into which Steven could impart different versions of himself and his father. Roy was Arnold, the father who absented himself, but he was also the young Steven, desperate to escape from the sexual battleground of his parents, and from his ethnic identity.

Afterward, he was rueful about the flight of the father. "I couldn't have made *Close Encounters* today," a more paternal Spielberg would say in 1994, "because I would never leave my family."[6]

In this anesthetized environment, the other "dreamer" is little Barry, the Good Kid, drawn like Neary to the unknown. The son of a single mother played by Melinda Dillon—open to the paranormal, hence portrayed sympathetically—he is encased in magic, half earthling, half extraterrestrial. His introduction to the wondrous and inexplicable is a Christmas-like Ark of the Torah epiphany: toys and appliances come to life, the train chugging, the monkey beating his drum, the refrigerator disgorging its contents, to all of which Barry responds with unflappable delight, much as the girl in *Poltergeist* accepts the voices from the television set. Magic and reality are not yet separate categories.

But with his bland saucer eyes, his zombielike stare, his ageless robotoxed face, the unblinking Barry is already half-alien to begin with. Possessed children were in vogue. *The Exorcist* had broken records in 1973, and just before that, Spielberg had directed his own demonic kid story in a television movie of the week, *Something Evil* (1972), an interesting little movie, with Sandy Dennis as an artist mother whose son is possessed. (Hmm.)

Roy's is meant to be a fairy-tale ending; he becomes, in Spielberg's words, "a real person. He loses his strings, his wooden joints, and . . . makes the most important decision in the history of the world."[7] That decision has to retain an aura of mystery, as Spielberg himself realized when Columbia induced him to shoot the interior of the spaceship for an anniversary reissue of the film on DVD. The new ending was in return for expensive additions and changes he wanted to make. In the new "director's cut," all that had been strange and mysterious was reduced to the banal and the ordinary, Roy in a track suit entering a generic getaway ship—lights flashing without being illuminating. The DVD now includes both versions.

Reviews were mostly favorable, though many critics (myself included) were put off by the heavy merchandising and the endless money stories; others simply were not captivated. Truffaut, who had been a figure of reverence on the set, was one of the movie's most astute analysts. He was fascinated (and alarmed) by the whole process, the extravagance, the difficulty. Initially, he had been concerned about playing the part, being neither an actor nor a believer in UFOs. "The only close encounters I have ever had are with women, children or books."[8]

But he pinpointed as well as anyone Spielberg's gift for giving "plausibility to the extraordinary." This he attributed to the director's care "in shooting all the scenes of everyday life to give them a slightly fantastic aspect while also, as a form of balance, giving the most everyday possible quality to the scenes of fantasy."

To Spielberg's huge disappointment, *Close Encounters* wasn't even nominated for an Academy Award. The nominees for 1977 (a banner year for women in a particularly lean era) were *Annie Hall* (the winner), *The Goodbye Girl* (for which Dreyfuss won Best Actor), *Julia*, *Star Wars*, and *The Turning Point.* Though always gracious to his friend Lucas in public, he felt that *Star Wars* had stolen his thunder. The irony is that at an early screening of *Star Wars* for pals, everyone thought it was going to tank. Everyone except Spielberg, who predicted that it would make a hundred million (an underestimate). The two were on the same wavelength. In their nostalgia for the sci-fi films, the Westerns, the TV shows (and books) of adolescence, they were out to create, or refashion, a peculiarly American set of myths.

To that end, what could be more fitting than that the two would join forces to make a movie that would resurrect the adventure serials of the forties and fifties, with a Cary Grant– or Humphrey Bogart–type hero, and featuring tiny thirties-style planes crossing wide swaths of maps.

But first there was *1941*.

7

1941 *and* Raiders of the Lost Ark

A WOULD-BE COMEDY about a Japanese attack on Los Angeles in World War II, *1941* was good-boy Steven's delayed descent into a variant of counterculture anarchy. He had paid his dues in the relatively buttoned-down nine-to-five world of Universal Studios, while the rest of the film brats were taking a beach break after film school and planning their stealth attack on Hollywood. If Paul Schrader's famous axiom about the drug-fueled era holds true—"If you remember the sixties, you weren't there"—then Spielberg wasn't there. His way of making up for lost time was to cut loose not with drugs but with cinematic mayhem.

Loosely based on several real incidents that followed the Japanese attack on Pearl Harbor in December 1941, the script by Bob Gale and Robert Zemeckis channeled the Angelinos' panic into slapstick farce. The pileup of mayhem, described as *Animal House* Goes to War, starred Dan Aykroyd, John Belushi,

Robert Stack, Slim Pickens, and Toshirô Mifune as commander of a submarine trained on Los Angeles.[1]

Initially, Hollywood's true wild man, macho, gun-loving John Milius, was going to direct the movie. He loved the black comedy for "its healthy sense of social irresponsibility."[2] So irresponsible was the project that when Spielberg took over and sent the script to Charlton Heston and John Wayne, both turned down the part of the general that Stack wound up playing, and Wayne urged Spielberg not to make such an unpatriotic film.

Spielberg and Wayne? First back up a bit. Steven had met the Bobs, Gale and Zemeckis, several years earlier, when they'd come to him with a student film. He had been so impressed that he'd produced their parody of Beatlemania, *I Wanna Hold Your Hand* (1978), in which a group of Jersey kids come to scream and faint over their idols, who never actually appear in the film. This was the first of many examples of Spielberg's encouragement and sponsorship of young talents, as well as an early display of Zemeckis's gifts as a vertigo-inducing cinematic prestidigitator. (He would go on to make *Back to the Future*, *Forrest Gump*, *Cast Away*, *Flight*, and the World Trade Center high wire act *The Walk*). Nineteen seventy-eight was also the year of *Animal House* and college humor and toga parties, with *Newsweek* featuring John Belushi's manic Bluto, that pin-up of screw-up, on its cover. Now this trio joined forces with Milius and began performing some frat club antics on their own, creating and documenting what turned out to be a kind of dry run—or dry heave—for the upcoming film. They would hang out at a joint called Tommie's, scarfing chili and staging food and vomit battles, which Spielberg filmed with an 8 mm camera. Where was Tommie's? On the road to the Oak Tree Gun Club, where the merry band of brothers shot skeet. Yes, you read that right. A little known fact about Spielberg is that he belonged to a gun club and was a fine shot, one of many Hollywood liberals who would prefer to keep this credential off their CVs. In his 1995 autobiography, Heston blew the whistle: "I suspect, in fact, that there are more filmmakers who are closet gun enthusiasts than there are closet homosexuals. Steven Spielberg has one of the finest gun collections in California but never refers to it, and never shoots publicly."[3] Why, he wondered, would the most famous filmmaker be worried about his reputation?

What did Amy Irving think of this boisterous buddy behavior? Steven had met and fallen in love with the brown-haired beauty, seven years his junior, while making *Close Encounters.* They were living together, but it was a sometimes awkward fit: she was a child of the theater, her mother an actress and her father Jules Irving, who had been the artistic director of the Repertory Theatre at Lincoln Center in New York. Moreover, she was at the beginning of her career, while Spielberg was an established celebrity. She felt she couldn't take roles in his films even if he wanted her to—she dreaded the charges of nepotism she knew firsthand as Jules Irving's daughter. She wanted to do it on her own. In addition, their world revolved around films—his films, his obsessions, his film friends (she once complained that they only went to dinner with studio heads). He was single-minded, incapable of real intimacy, mistrustful.

Julia Phillips describes his chagrin when Amy visited him on the set of *Close Encounters.* "I wish she hadn't come. She keeps crying and I keep wanting to say, 'Don't you understand, I'm fucking my movie.'"[4]

It wasn't even a double life, more like a triple one: while he was having his first intense love affair, he was hanging out with the guys, getting a lot of stupidity and aggression out of his system in the group high jinks he himself described as "a demolition derby." If Zemeckis, Gale, and Milius happily rode a whirlwind of destruction, Steven had his own delirious memories of childhood pandemonium. Chief of these was young Steve's "experiments" with his mother's blender, leaving the kitchen covered in slop—a primal scene that would lurk behind similar debacles in many of his films, most recently inspiring the refrigerator disgorging its contents in *Close Encounters.*

Now imagine that kitchen blender as a movie set, with lots of money to spend on bigger and more colorful ingredients, and you'll have a picture of the big-budget detonation that got out of hand, a film that, he realized in the middle of shooting, "was directing me, I wasn't directing it."[5]

He had initially wanted to make a "little film"—a desire to which he would give ever more rueful and futile utterance throughout his career—but was dissuaded by the screenwriters ("anyone can direct a little film; we want you to do big films"). Even Universal and Columbia, as joint producers, were ready to open the spigots for the hugely successful director. This is the point at which making an expensive flop was preferable to commissioning a small independent film—and sometimes, paradoxically, more profitable, as advertising, which was hugely expensive, was a disproportionate burden on little films. It has to do with budget size and opening date, an expanding number in an expanding season. Better to try for a Spielberg megahit and risk a flop than go to bat for an Altman film that might be a success. For one thing, the so-called flop might very well go on to recover its losses in the increasingly important international market, while Altman's "success" was measured in a different coinage.

The difficulties escalated from the start, and nuance went out the window. As did character. And budget. And social context. And the kind of crafting of jokes, with setups and releases, that went into silent comedy. Looney Tunes legend Chuck Jones was an early adviser, and the movie was like a two-hour Road Runner cartoon that never stopped to catch its breath. The Three Stooges were another model, enacting a fantasy of total destruction. It was *Hellzapoppin'* with no topical jokes (the Broadway version had opened with Hitler speaking Yiddish), *Laugh-In* with no laughs.

Once again—borrowing from the cartoon model—the rambunctious frenzy that works in a short space of time becomes belabored and annoying in a feature film. There were big scheduling problems with Aykroyd and Belushi, who were back and forth doing *Saturday Night Live*, and rampant cocaine use brought further delays. One day Belushi arrived late and drugged up. "You can do this to anyone else but you can't do it to me," Spielberg said, whereupon he assigned associate producer Janet Healy to babysit him and make sure he got to the shoot on time, with his lines memorized.[6] There were expensive sets, and miniatures, and planes crashing on a fictitious Hollywood Boulevard during Christmas. Oh yes, Christmas again: the Japanese conveniently attacked on young Spielberg's loved and hated holiday, and one of *1941*'s most prominent special effects was a huge illuminated Santa Claus like the one his family used to drive to see in New Jersey. At one point Saint Nicholas gets a profane update when the statue falls on a parachuting Belushi, so that the comedian's head emerges from Santa's body.

Other Spielberg themes and motifs are rolled out, like the "virgin-whore" split between the tomboy gal pal (who wants to learn about planes) and the exaggerated babe-bombshell. In a take-off on *Jaws*, the opening scene of a skinny-dipping woman clutching the upthrusting periscope of a surfacing Japanese submarine actually employs Susan Backlinie, who provided delectable shark bait in the earlier film.

The previews were terrible, so Spielberg, bypassing the premiere, went with Amy Irving on an extended trip to Japan, where they announced plans to marry after four years of living together.

The critics were merciless. Even the dependably mild-mannered and pan-averse Charles Champlin of the *Los Angeles Times* eviscerated the movie for its contempt and nihilism.[7] Nevertheless, like so many of Spielberg's "flops," it went on to become a cult movie in a restored version. Even at the time, it made a profit, especially abroad, where filmgoers in other countries relished the ugly portrait of America. Spielberg was embarrassed by this development—was Wayne right after all?—but the overseas audiences had a point, because Spielberg had always admired the soldiers of World War II who had fought and lost their lives on foreign soil, and that respect carried with it a kind of contempt or shame for his and his generation's belatedness, a nonparticipant's guilt.

The stories his father had told him were of heroes. Yet here were he and his fellow filmmakers, untested by war, and living and working in a place that was more about money than mettle. Hence this fairly savage portrait of self-regarding Hollywood, a community that has never endured battle but sees itself as the center of the universe—a satirical thrust that gets lost in the movie's unrelenting bedlam.

There's the guy desperately wanting to wear a uniform (shades of the faux pilot in *Catch Me If You Can*), going to a Jewish haberdasher. And the strangely likable enemy captain played by Toshirô Mifune), who in turn looks ahead to the sympathetic Japanese commander in *Empire of the Sun*, his stoical dignity contrasting with the unhinged hysteria of everyone else. Spielberg's hunger to identify, to take on some of the burden and responsibility of war, would lead to other, greater films about war—*Saving Private Ryan*, *Empire of the Sun*, *Schindler's List*.

The idea for *Raiders of the Lost Ark*, a remake of and tribute to the charmingly tacky adventure serials of the thirties and forties, originated with George Lucas, who shared it with his friend when the two men were on vacation in Hawaii. It sounded like fun, just what Steven needed in the depressing aftermath of *1941*. He was unhappy not just over the failure of the film but also because the relationship with Amy Irving had come to an end. No sooner had they disclosed plans to marry than, while the couple was still in Japan, these plans were abruptly canceled. Amy decamped to Santa Fe to live alone and regroup.

Earlier that year, she had made a movie in Texas, *Honeysuckle Rose*. She may have had an affair with her costar Willie Nelson, but in any case she had experienced a welcome new sense of herself, away from Steven and the film community of LA. Spielberg felt the dissolution keenly, realizing that it was a kind of delayed adolescent heartbreak. He'd been too caught up in making movies to go through the usual crushes and breakups, so it was as if this thirty-something man was feeling romantic loss for the first time.

Raiders of the Lost Ark was meant as "rehab" after the mindless extravagance of *1941*, penance in the form of submitting to George Lucas as producer. Because they liked and respected each other, they decided to bypass an agent, coming up with a complicated and vastly profitable deal whose primary feature was to give them a lot of money up front and eliminate distribution fees and other charges that took fifty percent of the gross. After the initial outrage of the studios and yearlong negotiations with Paramount, they got a lot of what they wanted, and in return they readily acceded to huge penalties if they went over budget. The large sum up front would be Spielberg's template for contracts to come, and would rarely be agreed upon without protracted arguments and negotiations.

Although the project took a long time to go into production, one of its happiest consequences was the acquisition of two people who would be Spielberg's key associates in the years to come. Frank Marshall, whom Steven had met in 1974, came on board as producer of *Raiders* and of most of his films thereafter. Marshall was someone who could supervise budgets, worry about costs, maintain momentum, but also, crucially, protect Spielberg from the interference of studio heads. The second professional ally was Kathleen Kennedy, who would become Marshall's wife after working with him on *Raiders.* She developed a strategy for keeping track of Steven's ideas—the bits of paper, words jotted here and there, images drawn on the fly—which she would collate into books.

There were the usual false starts, and eventually Lawrence Kasdan was hired to write the screenplay. A writer of TV commercials who would go on to write and direct *The Big Chill* and *Grand Canyon,* Kasdan had written a screwball love story called *Continental Divide* that Spielberg had liked. Kasdan figured they wanted someone "who could write *Raiders* in the same way that Hawks would have someone write a movie for him—a strong woman character, a certain kind of hero."[8] One envisions a pair resembling the nerdy paleontologist and his tormentor played by Cary Grant and Katharine Hepburn in *Bringing Up Baby.*

By the time the movie finally got under way—Steven had almost lost interest, it took so long—the hero played by Harrison Ford, originally intended to be a Cary Grant figure, was more a conventional action figure with a cynical Humphrey Bogart overlay. The two sides coexist without ever quite meshing. Indy is an adventure-loving scholar, but he's actually quite brutal, a grave-robbing imperialist mercenary looting Third World cultures and killing the natives.

Yet *Raiders'* tongue-in-cheek amoral cartoon style rendered such objections moot, seducing audiences into accepting its amorality and Indy as heroic. After *1941* Spielberg lamented that he wasn't good at comedy—not quite true. Perhaps he couldn't make a movie that was all comedy, and certainly he had no feeling for human slapstick, but his comic touch is unique, deft, reliable. Wit and humor (and charm) play a crucial part in all his films, not just as comic relief but as an integral ingredient, a buoyant element threaded through the most hair-raising stories, and disarming the audience when things get rough.

He and Lucas were nevertheless sensitive to charges of excesses of violence and bloodshed, and of racial stereotyping. And the putative Hawksian woman, Karen Allen as Indiana's Marion Ravenwood, Indy's on-again-off-again love interest and sometime ally, is another deglamorized Spielberg woman, a cartoonish gin-slinging tomboy who will soon be wearing dresses and screaming for help.

The transformation of intellectual into swaggering action hero and spitfire dame into an exaggeration of femininity dovetails with the ever-present motif of threatened masculinity, maleness that must prove itself. But Spielberg is in on the joke; the tone is mock-heroic. "Show a little backbone," Indy's pilot pal shouts to the frightened hero, who, in a sweet moment of sexual innuendo, discovers he is surrounded by snakes in the cockpit. Enter the Superman doppelgänger theme. The social awkwardness of Dr. Jones's sensitive fuddy-duddy absent-minded professor must be exaggerated before being usurped by the authority of Indy. (Karen Allen even resembles Margot Kidder, who played Lois Lane to Christopher Reeve's Superman in 1978.)

Raiders opened in June 1981, became the year's top-grossing film, and remains one of the highest-grossing films ever made. This time, the Academy spoke with forked tongue: once again Spielberg was snubbed as director, but the movie got nine nominations, including Best Picture (*Chariots of Fire* won).

Spielberg had gotten what he wanted. The fiasco of *1941* not only had curbed his financial hubris but had also made him artistically wary. His newfound caution was made to order for the business model of the eighties, in which a movie was no longer just a movie but a product line, a formula, a franchise that could be endlessly reproduced. Paramount signed the directors to a five-picture Indiana Jones deal. *Raiders of the Lost*

Ark, which would be renamed *Indiana Jones and the Raiders of the Lost Ark*, led to three more Indy films with a fifth in preproduction, a television series, *The Young Indiana Jones Chronicles* (1992–93), and numerous video games.

Appearing when it did, the movie came to be considered a sort of bellwether of the Reagan era, with its patriotism and good humor, a welcome relief from raucous anti-American anti-Hollywood rhetoric and loose-cannon auteurs. Simplistic dichotomies were in the air, like "films" versus "movies"—the former laboriously off-putting or attractively challenging, the latter popcorn-fun or popcorn-trivial, depending on your point of view, a schism that would be articulated in the Tom Shone–Blockbuster vs. Peter Biskind–art film divide. "It's only a movie," was the mantra. But it's-only-a-movie movies didn't win Academy Awards. Until they did.

Time magazine had heralded the shift in taste in a 1977 article on *Star Wars:* what a "weird idea to make a movie whose only idea was to give pleasure," wrote the reporter with heavy irony, pointing to downers like *Chinatown* (and no doubt implying such thrillingly pessimistic early-seventies gems as *The Conversation*, *Klute*, *Night Moves*, *Nashville*, and *Dog Day Afternoon*).[9] As if there were not many forms of pleasure, not limited to the instant high of refined sugar.

Raiders was a B movie with A movie ambitions, poised to make the leap. It was meant to hark back to the "fun" movies of an earlier period, but for all its economy of budget and shooting time, it had the usual Spielberg epic reach, the romps and car chases and death-defying moments of the serials now expanded into an effortful 115 minutes. It was thus a far cry from studio pictures back in the day, when even the "prestige" films were expeditious in comparison.

The nostalgia—this wistful mythologizing of a synthetic past—is not just for old movies but for the young selves that loved them. Lucas and Spielberg are walking encyclopedias of the pop culture of their youth and even antecedent to it, but they create a mythology of the past that doesn't rely on familiarity with the sources. Packaged for a new audience that is ready to enter a prolonged childhood, the pastiche of adventure serials—toy planes and maps and buried treasure—could be endlessly reproduced.

Raiders had its heavyweight champions: an unstinting Vincent Canby of the *New York Times* called it "one of the most deliriously funny, ingenious and stylish American adventure movies ever made."[10]

In the shift in values of which the movie itself was a prime mover, *Raiders of the Lost Ark* was admitted in 1999 to the U.S. Library of Congress's National Film Registry, deemed "culturally, historically, or aesthetically significant."

8

E.T., Poltergeist, *and* Twilight Zone

As HE WAS MAKING the film, and not for the first time in his career, Spielberg wasn't sure exactly what *E.T.* was. He told one interviewer that he went back and forth, thinking sometimes it was a personal film about the effects of divorce and at other times a kiddie show that would be unreleasable in movie theaters and would have to play on Saturday morning television next to *He-Man* and *Transformers*.

Typically, he would start out thinking he wanted to do one thing—*Close Encounters* was going to be a "political thriller"—and end up doing something else altogether, an unconventional hybrid. The early version of *E.T.* was a script by John Sayles called *Night Skies*, a reworking of John Ford's *The Searchers*, in which a farm family is terrorized by alien invaders instead of Indians. Among other drawbacks, the dastardliness of the invaders would have been uncongenial to a director who, outside of the cartoon villains of the action films, was incapable of see-

Home phoned: E.T. and Elliott (Henry Thomas).
Universal Pictures/Photofest

ing anyone as pure evil, least of all the otherworldly creatures who had fired his childhood imagination.

Spielberg would always maintain, a bit disingenuously, that he didn't have a "personal style"; he was no Welles imposing his vision on his material, but a journeyman who could work in every genre. Even aside from the sheer virtuosity of the filmmaking, his movies were more personal than many of the films of his edgier contemporaries. The very difficulties he had, initially, in arriving at what a film was about came from his compulsion to insert versions of his own family drama into the more ritualized conventions of genres where family ordinarily took a back seat. For the most part, science fiction and action movies stay away from romantic or domestic entanglements: it's the whole point, and it's why they are called escapist. But from families, there is no escape. Spielberg manages to combine escapism and inescapability, no mean feat, and you can see him feeling his way toward this combination, finding the balance he wants.

Eventually, this is precisely what pulled in audiences. "Spielberg was succeeding while Disney films were failing," *Variety*'s Art Murphy pointed out, "because Spielberg was willing to acknowledge the harsh reality of divorce and incorporate it into his narrative world."[1]

The family in science fiction was there primarily to be traumatized by the terrors from outer space, just as the audience is there to have its mind blown by special effects. With Spielberg the family has its own importance and urgency, a sense of life being lived quite apart from the otherworldly theme. His other genre-crossing strategy was to integrate into ordinary reality a cartoon ethic and aesthetic—the child/animal/outsider's point of view, the abrupt juxtapositions and tonal shifts, the easy leap from physical to metaphysical and back again.

Spielberg, like most of us, straddles two worlds, two views of the family: the child's wish to escape and the grown-up's yearning to go back to some idealized version of family. Most of us "move on," escape the family by growing up, moving away, and creating a new one—often some kind of revised version, or antiversion—of the one we've left behind. Men feel obliged to answer the question that plagues the protagonist of *Close Encounters:* To Be or Not To Be . . . a Father. But Steven, Hamlet-like, remains stuck in a kind of undecided but artistically fertile equipoise, a past that is always present.

Not only his childhood but whatever he was feeling and experiencing at any given time went into his films. Right now, the thirty-four-year-old filmmaker was having a letdown after *Raiders.* It hadn't provided the outlet he needed for his imagination, nor did it take place in that real-world setting from which that imagination could take its leaps. In addition, during the shooting, he had felt isolated and lonely. His then-girlfriend

Kathleen Carey was halfway around the world, and he began remembering how he felt as a ten-year-old and longed for a playmate he could talk to and who—even more crucially—would listen to him.

The script was by Melissa Mathison, whom Spielberg met on the set of *Indiana Jones*. (She was Harrison Ford's girlfriend at the time. She would die of cancer in 2015, but not before writing another Spielberg script: *The BFG*—Big Friendly Giant—adapted from a Roald Dahl story and scheduled to open in 2016.) Her only previous credit was a rewrite of *The Black Stallion*, but she and Steven had an instant affinity. They began sharing all manner of confidences, not least of which was the movie Spielberg wanted to make next. She instinctively grasped what he was trying to do. He had a soft spot he was afraid to show. "He kept fretting that *E.T.* was too soft," Mathison told a reporter, "until finally he stopped worrying about pleasing the men in the audience."[2] Spielberg felt their relationship was symbiotic: "Melissa is 80% heart and 20% story logic. It took her sensitivity and my know-how to make *E.T.* Besides, I work better with women. I claim no profound understanding of women, but I have an agreeable faith in them."

E.T., made for very little compared to the escalating costs and uncertainties of *Close Encounters*, would turn out to be the "most emotionally complicated and least technically complicated" film he'd made to date.[3] For a cameraman he wanted someone who was hungry and would work fast, and went to Allen Daviau, who had shot *Amblin'*. E.T. himself, the BEM (bug-eyed monster in sci-fi lingo), was the work of Italian artist and sculptor Carlo Rambaldi, whom Spielberg brought over after a $700,000 spaceman effort by the special effects crew had failed. As Spielberg said, "E.T. could not only look sad, but he could look curiously sad." He was meant to be wizened, not beautiful, and for the all-important eyes, his models were Einstein, Carl Sandburg, and Ernest Hemingway.[4] The creature was certainly no beauty, and he could terrify children: those gnarled pokey fingers like the witch in Hansel and Gretel, the wrinkled oversize head bearing an eerie resemblance, as an art critic noted, to Munch's *The Scream.*

E.T. was an Ugly Duckling story—the Jewish kid with the long nose and big ears, misfit in Arizona's Wasp and jock culture, transformed by cinematic magic into a big-headed extraterrestrial, cousin to the childlike figures who had descended from the spaceship in *Close Encounters of the Third Kind.* And a lonely guy story: Spielberg told *Rolling Stone* interviewer Michael Sragow that he thought of E.T. as the Nowhere Man from the Beatles song.[5] The alien would be the pal and soul mate of another lonely guy figure of isolation. Imagining himself as a ten-year-old—which by his own admission he still was—he brooded over the need for a friend "who needed me as much as I needed him."

The lonely child—who hasn't been one? The imaginary playmate—who hasn't had one? The Nowhere Land, who hasn't lived there? The movie touched millions and showed just how deeply in tune with his audience Spielberg was. He was in the process not of "finding" an audience but of creating one magnetically, unrestricted by age or language or even gender. The intensity of a child's longing was a universal experience; the search for a soul mate, for one's "other half," the classic definition of love. Through this magical twinning, Spielberg himself was moving toward adult acceptance rather than defiance. "Why don't you grow up? Think how other people feel for a change," the older brother scolds Elliott when a casual remark about their father has wounded their mother.

If *Close Encounters* had revolved around the flight of the father from domesticity, seen from the adult's point of view, *E.T.* was a story of reconciliation told from the child's viewpoint, a boy's return to the family out of a stronger sense of self.

The little sister (Drew Barrymore, in a stunning performance) is still the mother's darling; the older brother has his pack of teenage buddies, already masking their feelings with crude humor. Elliott is the lost middle child, but when he sneaks E.T. into his bedroom and starts introducing him to his toys, he has finally found someone to whom his world is important, who will greet his stories with neither skepticism nor indifference. And however genderless E.T. may appear, Elliott is the decider. When little sister asks whether the weird-looking asexual and ageless playmate is a boy or a girl, Elliott quickly and preemptively cries, "Boy!"

From the opening in the forest, and the mysterious appearance of the abandoned E.T., the movie exudes an air of enchantment, of extrasensory mystery that is nevertheless rooted in nature and the Arizona landscape. Another cartoon image resonates: from *Pinocchio*, when Jiminy Cricket arrives on the mountaintop at night, surveys the town below, its grid of lights twinkling like stars. The suburban vista of look-alike houses, now seen from the child's (and E.T.'s) point of view, has a magic of its own. There's no we-versus-them mentality as there was in *Close Encounters*. Even the grown-ups and the lumbering, literal-minded officials—scientists and security personnel, in hazmat suits with jangling keys—are simply creatures from another world. As seen, waist down, from a child's point of view; they are too far from the ground—or their own childhood—to *see*. Even the mother—a sympathetic Dee Wallace—is simply too harried to notice the alien in the household.

Elliott, by contrast, is so in tune with his pal that he will feel his feelings, experience his drunkenness, merge with him. Through the strengthening of this bond, he will evolve from the need to possess E.T. ("I have absolute power," he tells brother Michael) to the deeper, freer love of letting him go. Their parting at the end is—depending on your point of view (and like many such Spielberg scenes)—either overwhelmingly moving or squirmingly overlong. The novelist Martin Amis, an admirer, is of the first mind, and eloquently describes Spielberg's gift. "As an artist Spielberg is a mirror, not a lamp. His line to the common heart is so direct that he unmans you with the frailty of your own defences, and the transparency of your most intimate fears and hopes."[6]

While worrying about *E.T.* being too "soft" for men in the audience, Spielberg wound up captivating them instead. As with *Jaws*, men especially could experience both the pleasure and the terror of an unmanning. Denied that particular catharsis I felt artery-clogged by the long good-bye, which creates a sort of stasis, affirming the superiority of the child's unfettered imagination over the limited and spiritually downtrodden adult.

With his imagination cleansed of perverse longings and adult desires, Elliott is stuck in preadolescence. Spielberg can't negotiate the passage from sweet, flirty Elliott—in a sparkling scene he dances with his blond classmate in incandescent imitation of John Wayne and Maureen O'Hara in *The Quiet Man*—to horny teenager.

If you had to pin down the theology behind Spielberg's articles of narrative faith—hope, optimism, and a belief in goodness triumphant—they are actually closer to a Mormon worldview than a Christian or Jewish one. Mormon writers gravitate to genre fiction like fantasy, sci-fi, and children's literature, as Mark Oppenheimer reported in an article in the *New York Times*, and wonder "if their culture militates against more highbrow writing."[7] Shannon Hale, an author of young adult fiction, observes that Jewish writers have made a large impact in literary fiction, much of which tends to exalt the tragic or the gloomy, but Mormons, whose culture prefers the sunny and optimistic, have not. Such portrayals of hope and goodness, Hale says, "can ring false in a literary world." Like Steven Spielberg's own aversion to murkiness and ambiguity, Mormon stories (see Stephanie Meyers), are driven by crystal clear plots, avoiding sex and other pleasurable (or sinful) aspects of adult life—smoking, drinking, and pessimism.

But there are chinks in the Boy Scout façade, glimpses of carnality in Spielberg that are visible only to those with a keen eye for visual innuendo. Andrew Sarris provides a deliciously twisty reading of an incipient relationship between Elliott's mother and "Keys," the government scientist played by Peter Coyote, the one adult who "gets" E.T. and becomes Elliott's friend. Initially he is seen as threatening and gets his nickname because of the keys hanging from his belt. Sarris observes that in the end, as they watch E.T.'s spaceship depart, the two adults are linked together visually. Because it was done without words, "only children and Freudians can make the crucial connections between the telltale keys fondled near the crotch of the potential father figure and the displaced phallus represented by E.T. himself."[8] The further implication for the Freudians among us is that maybe the kids, far from being complete sexual innocents, are onto something that passes over our heads.

Until Spielberg bears down on our emotions, usually with the help of John Williams's swelling musical cues, the movie is full of wistful undertones, contrapuntal emotions, complex moods, and wit. E.T. assembling a phone is the amateur son's playful rebuke to the engineer father. A sense of shared loss and a growing comradeship between the brothers emerges when the two come upon their father's possessions and remember the smell and feel of him.

Spielberg himself was in fact moving forward with a sense of well-being owing to his relationships, both with Kathleen Carey and with the children on the set. Possibly because of his charmed interactions with the kids, he was discovering—even anticipating—the joys of fatherhood. This he expected to experience by marrying Kathleen, with whom he'd found a kind of emotional openness he'd never had before. There was, he discovered, a life outside of film!

The response to *E.T.* was overwhelming. Reviews were ecstatic—Michael Sragow called Spielberg a "space age Jean Renoir," and some embraced it as a religious parable, or as we always seem bound to say, a "quasi-religious parable." McBride suggests that Universal encouraged such an interpretation, with "ads showing E.T.'s glowing finger touching the hand of a child, evoking Michelangelo's Sistine Chapel image of God's finger touching the hand of Adam."[9] Spielberg admitted sheepishly that he and Mathison had thought they might be getting into "sticky" religious areas in the moment when E.T. is on the bicycle in a white hospital robe (echoes of the young Spielberg playing Jesus on his Jersey porch) and his "immaculate" heart is glowing. "We already knew this coming back to life was a form of resurrection. But I'm a nice Jewish boy from Phoenix, Arizona. If I ever went to my mother and said, 'Mom, I've made this movie that's a Christian parable,' what do you think she'd say? She has a kosher restaurant on Pico and Doheny in Los Angeles."[10]

Shortly after the film's release in June 1982, Spielberg was reportedly earning as much as half a million dollars *per day* as his share of the profits. *E.T.* dethroned *Star Wars* and was so successful that it moved Spielberg from celebrity director to household name, all of which may have compensated for its loss of the Best Picture Oscar to *Gandhi.* His mother, now ensconced in the delicatessen business with her new husband, took time off to appear, with great panache, on the Johnny Carson show. There were two hundred authorized product tie-ins and thousands of rip-offs, with lawsuits to follow; charges of exploitation and charges of plagiarism. Spielberg felt exposed as never before. The ultimate cashing-in would be one of the biggest tourist attractions ever, an *E.T.* ride installed at Universal in 1991.

The Mr. Hyde side of the Spielberg persona lurking in the jettisoned Sayles script got a workout in *Poltergeist,* which

Spielberg produced at the same time as *E.T.* "*Poltergeist* is what I fear and *E.T.* is what I love."[11] The nastiness and ghoulishness had to come out by proxy. Though Tobe Hooper was the nominal director, it was Spielberg who made most of the decisions and was on the set every day. Eyewitnesses spread the word that Spielberg had directed, reports that seriously hurt Hooper's career.

The Spielberg building blocks are all here—the Norman Rockwell suburban neighborhood, this time ironically called Questa Verde Estates, built on top of an ancient Indian burial ground, and under siege from vengeful spirits of displaced Native Americans. There's the tree from Steven's New Jersey childhood, with its malevolent branches; voices from the people inside the TV that only a little girl can see and hear; messy childhood closets that themselves become sources of terror.

Continuing as producer, the "bad" Steven, the mischief maker enamored of the ghoulish and nasty, found a kindred spirit in Joe Dante, director of a low-budget werewolf film Spielberg had liked. Spielberg saw everything, had an eye for talent, and, remembering his own early struggles, was eager to mentor young directors. Dante credited him with salvaging his career. *Gremlins*, the movie he asked Dante to direct (from a script by Chris Columbus), was a parody of Spielberg adorableness, which he called "*E.T.* with teeth."[12]

Dante teamed with Spielberg and John Landis for their next project, an omnibus movie derived from episodes from *The Twilight Zone.* Dante's "It's a Good Life," with children turning into cartoon characters, proved to be the freshest and most original adaptation; George Miller's "Nightmare at 20,000 Feet," with a terrified passenger John Lithgow, the scariest. We can't know how Spielberg's original episode would have turned out if he hadn't shifted gears in midproject because of a tragedy on the set.

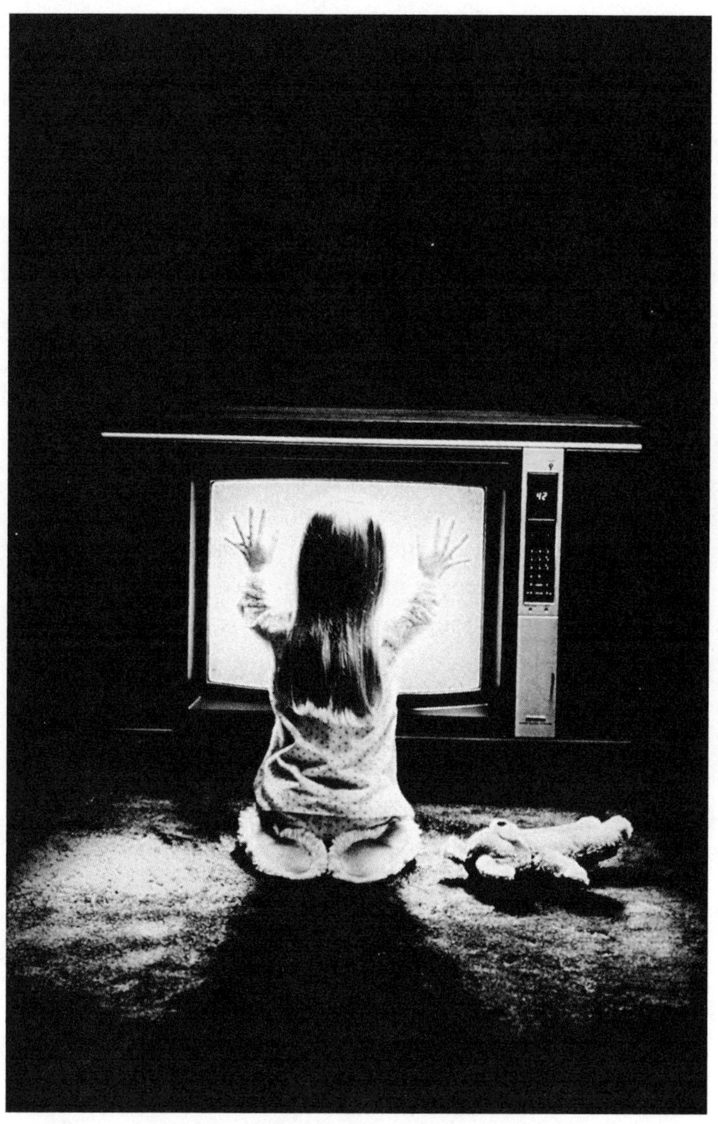

They're here: in *Poltergeist*, Carol Anne (Heather O'Rourke) receives messages from the television that only she can hear—as had a seven-year-old Spielberg. MGM/UA/Photofest

During a night shooting of Landis's segment, in which Vic Morrow's character rescues two Vietnamese children from a burning village, there was an explosion on the ground, their helicopter crashed into a tree, and all three were killed. The whole ghastly affair was handled the Hollywood way. Manslaughter charges were filed against the technical crew; a less than-thorough investigation ensued; and the trial got lost in a legal stew, while failing to indict the one unequivocal crime: the illegal hiring of children in violation of safety board rules.

There were enough black marks to go around. Spielberg managed to avoid investigation by signing a paper saying he hadn't been on the set, which seemed to satisfy the district attorney's office. Producer-friend Frank Kennedy, who had been present when the accident occurred, eluded investigation by leaving the country and simply being unavailable. John Landis was tried and acquitted. Spielberg escaped blame, but public outrage at the exoneration of Landis left a bad taste and may have colored Academy attitudes enough to affect the Best Picture vote. Landis bounced back in the way that Hollywood miscreants usually do. Spielberg had scuttled his original plan and ended up making "Kick the Can," a sentimental vignette featuring Scatman Crothers in an old folks home.

For Hollywood it was business as usual. Rather than pull the film, Warner Brothers not only went ahead and released it but, adding insult to injury, blamed the victims for taking the risk that killed them.

9

Indiana Jones and the Temple of Doom *and* The Color Purple

"If there is a dark side to me it will come out in one of my films."

How deeply was Steven Spielberg affected by the deaths on the set? He made a public statement after the accident describing the pall that had fallen on the 150 people working on the production, saying, "We are still just sick to the center of our souls."[1] If so, did this anguish (as some suggested) feed the theme of child endangerment and rescue in his next film, *Indiana Jones and the Temple of Doom?*

Not only does this violent and grisly movie feature a more mercenary Indiana Jones, who gets drugged and turns malevolent; the main adventure concerns kidnapping the children from an entire village. Lucas, the producer and story writer, set it before World War II in order to avoid having Nazi villains, so it took place in a remote Himalayan village in India.

Screenwriters Gloria Katz and Willard Huyck were hired. Spielberg and Lucas wanted a film that contrasted with the lightness of *Raiders of the Lost Ark*, and the couple complied. Although the movie has since risen in critics' estimation, because of its boldness and intensity—presumably an early foray into "immersion" filmmaking—there was very little in the movie's savagery to touch emotional chords. Its very excess bespeaks a kind of comic exaggeration, a grossout extravaganza that Vincent Canby called "exuberantly tasteless and entertaining," in which hearts are wrenched out of bodies, people roasted in a human barbecue.[2] Even the comic relief was unusually dark, not to mention the dinner fare: live snakes, fried beetles, eyeball soup, anyone?

Nineteen eighty-four turned out to be the year of the Two Naughty (not to say Sadistic) Spielbergs, as he also produced Joe Dante's *Gremlins*, a yuk-fest about a monster-spawning pet. So violent were these purportedly children-oriented films that the MPAA, at Spielberg's suggestion, would add another notch to the rating system, PG-13, parental guidance required for age thirteen and under—ironic, as it would seem to eliminate the one age group that might respond to the worms and snails and puppy dog tails that little boys are made of.

In alluding to the dark side of himself that forced its way into a film, he confessed, "They are almost cathartic for me."[3] Purified no doubt by the exorcism of his demons in the *Temple of Doom*, the director later disavowed the following *Indiana Jones and the Last Crusade*, saying he had been "consciously regressing."[4]

The general grimness of the film contrasts sharply with the wit and buoyancy of the opening scene, a stylishly staged Busby Berkeley–adventure film pastiche in a Chinese nightclub. A glittering Kate Capshaw sings "Anything Goes" in Mandarin, while an elegantly dinner-jacketed Ford bounces around and under tables trying to capture a diamond and a vial containing an antidote to a deadly poison he has swallowed courtesy of Chinese baddies. This is the last trace of real fun, as the movie quickly bogs down in a series of muddy, dark, skeleton-infested fright scenes. Ford will degenerate into sour and scruffy in no time, and this first important role for Capshaw, the director's future wife, will plummet into featherbrained helplessness. The voice that warbled Cole Porter quickly turns shrill, becoming Spielberg's most nerve-wracking version of the Shrieking Woman. At one point Ford, voicing audience exasperation, tells her to shut up.

Critics' dislike of the film came out in hostility toward Capshaw's character, and toward the actress herself, some even blaming her for the perceived failure of the movie. So visceral was the response that criticism of Spielberg's approach seemed to bleed into and encourage a shared misogyny. Gene Siskel, for example, complained about Capshaw's whimpering and said that when viewers see her "dangling over molten lava, . . . we wish she would fall in."[5]

The tortures designed for the actress were excessive even by the standards of the time. Could Spielberg be going overboard, torturing the sassy blond as if she were one of his kid sisters, because he was attracted to her? The beautician's daughter and aspiring actress from Missouri was the kind of all-American beauty that he had acknowledged a weakness for. "Maybe I've been searching for the ultimate shiksa," he told one interviewer.[6]

She had impressed the director when she came for an interview, and the feeling was mutual. Born Kathy Sue Nail in Fort Worth, Texas, she had married Robert Capshaw, her college sweetheart, a high school principal, and had a child with him, but had ambitions beyond the small-town Missouri where she now lived. Deceptively giggly, with a model's face and features (she actually had brown hair, but dyed it blond) and a sporty-flapper look, she had come to audition for Steven—literally for

Steven, in that she may have wanted a role in the film, but that was secondary to the designs she had on the man himself. The feeling was confirmed on sight . . . or perhaps one should say, "on smell."

"It was a smell of familiarity," she told Stephen Schiff in a *New Yorker* interview.[7]

This instant olfactory charge she likened to that of a blindfolded mother recognizing the smell of her newborn. He *belonged* to her. For Spielberg, the lure of "familiarity" would have hit the erotic sweet spot: an attraction rooted in childhood yearnings and inhibitions, one that takes on a delicious inescapability. A marriage thus formed can be an unconscious strategy for simultaneously violating and observing the incest taboo. As Adam Phillips has written, in one of his charming Freudian aphorisms, "If sex is the way out of the family, falling in love is the route back, the one-way ticket that is always a return."[8] Spielberg's mother was "more like a kid sister," and the director was ever prone to blurring the familial and the romantic in his kid-sister-like heroines. As the tomboyishly named Willie Scott, Kate had one fabulous scene, and was then subjected to the kind of torture offensive he'd perpetrated on his sisters to gain control in his woman-dominated home. Heat, snakes, bugs, darkness . . .

If the subsequent Indy films would temper the racism in response to negative critiques, the sexism remained unadulterated. If anything, the women became increasingly caricatured—subjected to less physical torture, but also less trustworthy and more villainous. That is, until Karen Allen returns safely as a mom in *Indiana Jones and the Kingdom of the Crystal Skull.*

But perhaps nothing would equal the distorting horrors perpetrated on the shrieking Capshaw that alienated reviewers. Could it be that the future husband—all unwitting—was trying to thwart his future wife's career before it began? (Hints of such a buried design will emerge in a 1994 showdown between the two over her career, a fateful encounter that happens to occur after they have just watched a television rerun of *Indiana Jones and the Temple of Doom.*)

In light of the Spielberg-Capshaw movie, one can't resist asking: how much of the violence against women in movies, the ubiquitous "turn-on" of gorgeous women being gleefully tormented, is a delayed revenge perpetrated by nerds on the high school beauties who wouldn't give them a backward glance? The Alfred Hitchcock syndrome: socially awkward, unprepossessing artist delights in finding ingenious ways to punish the women who have held a thwarted attraction.

The seventies and eighties were, in the eyes of many reviewing from a feminist perspective (Carrie Rickey and myself among others), a nadir for women in the movies. There were a few interesting roles, most of them played by Meryl Streep, Sissy Spacek, Sally Field, or Ellen Burstyn, but for the most part babes and sidekicks and sex objects ruled, and serious actresses, no longer having a studio behind them, went begging. The "cool" films of the seventies, from *The Godfather* on, were mostly male affairs, representing the nerdy unsexiness of the movie brats. The scene when Al Pacino's Michael explicitly excludes wife Kay (Diane Keaton) from a truth-telling family conference is the moment, as I once wrote, when *The Godfather* effectively "closed the door on wives, girlfriends and mothers at the very moment when the women's movement, on fire with a whole range of equity issues, was coming out of the closet and into the media spotlight."[9]

Only ten years previously, right after *The Sugarland Express,* Spielberg had given an interview that might have been cause for cheers. "I'd like to make a woman's picture," he told Andrew Borrow in *Filmmakers Newsletter,* "because the motion picture industry has systematically shied away from the woman's movie and there are few major roles in the works for the self-realized woman." He felt that he almost owed it to them, as they "shove[d] their men into the movie theaters each weekend."[10]

Yes, reader, once long ago, women were actually the deciders as to what movie a couple would see on a Saturday night, and Hollywood catered to their taste. Then the male-oriented action-adventure juggernaut got under way, and the "woman's picture" fell by the wayside. As his relationship with the women he worked with makes clear, Spielberg was no misogynist. It was just that he liked guy stuff more. And action, along with being hugely profitable, was, as Spielberg admitted in the same interview, both sensational and irresistible.

"I think one of the reasons a lot of directors fall back on the action motif is because they don't want to be bored during the three months of location filming. A laugh a minute or a stunt a minute is always very exciting. You know, controlling 100 cars or Mike Nichols controlling twenty B-25's [in *Catch-22*], or Stanley Kubrick sending thousands of French soldiers up the anthill [in *Paths of Glory*], it's a great feeling. There's something funny about the supercharged ego-drive of the action director. He wants to move mountains, not people."[11]

Except for the uptick in violence, the Indiana Jones movies are as old-fashioned as can be. Spielberg was going backward and forward at the same time, making a film about an irresponsible father at the age he was about to sire a son of his own. Amy Irving had come back into his life, putting on hold the flirtation between the director and the midwestern brunette-turned-blonde shiksa, who would in a few years convert to Judaism.

For the moment, Capshaw's timing was off: Irving had staged a surprise reunion in Sri Lanka, where Steven had gone to scout for locations. He was smarting from the breakup, but some love was still there, and the relationship resumed on a more solid footing: she'd earned acclaim for work on the stage and her supporting role in Barbra Streisand's *Yentl*. They were both more relaxed; she was more confident about her career, and he was able to take more of an interest in it. At a joyous celebration for Amy's thirty-first birthday in September 1984, she became pregnant. Steven participated in the pregnancy *couvade*-style, to the point of wanting to pick out baby clothes with her. He took her to the doctor's office in order to hear the unborn child's heartbeat. At one point, she said he was looking forward to the baby so he "would have somebody to share his toys with."[12] They waited until after Max was born, then married "like characters in a Frank Capra film, before a wise old judge." Spielberg felt that Max was going to change his life. The born-again Dad was going to drive home in rush-hour traffic to take his son to and from school. He would largely keep to his promise, leaving the office early, changing diapers, getting up at night with the baby.

Meanwhile, Steven was becoming downright seigneurial. In 1984, the same year he formed Amblin Entertainment with Frank Marshall and Kathleen Kennedy, he quit his offices at Warner Brothers to take possession of a vast compound that Universal Studios had built for him, just to keep their mogul happy and with no contractual obligations attached. He had also acquired a palatial new home in the Pacific Palisades. Its previous tenants included Douglas Fairbanks Jr., Cary Grant, and Barbara Hutton. The offices were created and the house remodeled in the southwestern style that reminded him of the Arizona landscape, which he had always loved, and Amy of her home in New Mexico. The incredibly lavish Santa Fe adobe-style office complex contained a forty-five-seat screening room, two editing rooms, a video arcade, a kitchen with a professional chef, a gym, an outdoor spa, gardens, and a wishing well with a miniature *Jaws* shark. Here he hung his movie posters and Norman Rockwell paintings. The garden was also wired with an intercom: visitors described strolling through the paths when—shades of those radio murmurings from childhood—voices would emanate from a rock or a tree, reminding

Steven of an appointment, or inquiring whether anyone would like a drink.

Home and office were where he spent his screen-watching time—which is to say most of his time when he wasn't working—so there were televisions in every room. He was a homebody, a couch potato, not a traveler. He admitted (boasted) that he would rather fall asleep watching TV than hearing the waters lapping the beach on the Riviera.

At the same time, to keep his options open, he remained in business with Steve Ross, big spender and legendary head of Warner Brothers, the powerhouse who'd taken an interest in him and whom he regarded as yet another surrogate father. They had met in 1981, when Spielberg was immediately smitten with the prepossessing producer, with his "silver screen charisma," whose flash and style seemed to come out of a Hollywood past. Ross, in turn, had had his own agenda: he was eager to get Spielberg to make as many films as possible for Warner's. The courtship included lavish favors on Ross's part, with reciprocal thank yous from Steven. This new "father" was teaching him tricks of the trade and how to handle his wealth.

In *Temple of Doom*, an irresponsible man has to redeem himself by rescuing the children, but Indy's redemption comes a little too late for conviction, in a movie 99 percent of whose energy comes from the lure of irresponsibility. Maybe *Indiana Jones* was Spielberg's last blowout of hyperjuvenilia. But even on the threshold of paternity, as his career was about to swerve into seriousness with *The Color Purple*, he produced two comedies about nerdy loser dads who have to be rescued by their children! *Goonies* (director Richard Donner, story by Spielberg), in which a gang of preteens discover hidden treasure and save Dad, was inspired by the time Steven and his buddies deliberately threw up in a movie theater. And then there was the glorious *Back to the Future*, a classic on the order of *Groundhog*

Day—with which it shares a twisty metaphysical view of time doubling back on itself. The Bobs, Gale and Zemeckis, were responsible for script and direction, but Spielberg's Amblin produced the film—he even makes a cameo appearance driving a jeep—and his childhood is everywhere on view, as is that all-too-rare gift for adult humor. In the movie's decidedly racy Oedipal twist, a mother and her son meet as contemporaries, as Leah Spielberg and her son felt themselves to be in so many ways. Michael J. Fox is Marty McFly, the rescuer-kid who, thanks to Christopher Lloyd's souped-up DeLorean, is hurtled back to 1955, where his future parents—wimp George (Crispin Glover) and juicy Lorraine (Lea Thompson)—are not likely to marry and give birth to him unless he does something fast. The movie slyly addresses every child's ontological questions: How did my parents get together? Do they belong together? And the Freudian "family romance" fantasy, are they really my parents? And—ultimate revenge—instead of being a mere accident of nature in the wake of adults' copulation, the child takes control of things, prearranges his birth by introducing father and mother. But in a delicate brush with incest, instead of falling for wimp George, the delectable Lorraine develops a passionate crush on adorable Marty. The brilliance of the movie is the way it delivers an adult frisson in the middle of a noisy and wacky kid-friendly sci-fi comedy. Perhaps only Spielberg could get away with this film's blurring of childhood and adult longings, the overlapping of innocence and experience.

Throughout his career there would be sightings of this unofficial Spielberg: the fratty Rover Boy of food-fight fame, the gun-owning marksman, the occasional smoker of cigarettes, the guy who laughs like hell at dirty jokes (and even makes a few), and perhaps most tantalizing, the tycoon who lives like one in not-quite-plain sight.

Meanwhile, the man with the Oedipal hang-ups was about to climb the next steep step, get some competition of his own in the form of a son. Time travel indeed! Like the character Tom Hanks would play in *Big* (1988), another age-changing comedy written by none other than Spielberg's sister Anne, and possibly—as many conjectured—inspired by her brother, Spielberg would grow up seemingly overnight.

With *The Color Purple*, the "real" world was knocking. The time had come for Spielberg to do his Irving Thalberg–Stanley Kramer turn. Before, a light had shone and a little kid had led them into the future, had reinvented the blockbuster and shown Hollywood how to reach its youngest, widest audience ever. But the light had brought more profits than prestige. Now another role opened before him—that of the socially responsible filmmaker. He wanted to make an adult film, something that would challenge him, he told a reporter, "to use a different set of muscles."

It was early in the shooting when Amy called to say the baby was on its way. Spielberg had deliberately moved the interiors to Universal Studios so he could be near home when the baby arrived. He responded to his wife's summons to come "direct" Max's delivery, which occurred on June 13, 1985. It so happened that Max entered the world at the same time that Spielberg was beginning to shoot the scene of Celie giving birth. The cries of her child emerging are those of Max, taped by the father while his son was being given a bath.

Cynical critics would jump on *The Color Purple*, an adaptation of Alice Walker's Pulitzer Prize–winning novel about blacks in the deep South in the thirties, as nothing more than a bid for the Oscar. But the move was a natural way for Spielberg to grow up, to reach out. The prestige film was as much a Hollywood staple as the action blockbuster, and at this point he was as much old Hollywood as new. He was thirty-seven. He now had a son. He would eventually say it was the birth of Max more than any other event in his life that pushed him toward a recognition of his Jewish identity, though that wouldn't become clear until the watershed of *Schindler's List*, and the interviews and stock-taking in its aftermath. For now, his identification with the oppressed took the form of an instinctive and long-standing sense of solidarity with blacks and the civil rights struggle.

The film might also have been a kind of unconscious compensation. If, like war, each film is in some ways a reaction to the one before, then perhaps *The Color Purple* was, as J. Hoberman suggested, "an apology for the rampant white male supremacism of Indiana Jones."[13]

But the risk was enormous. Not just the usual identity politics (how dare he, a white man . . . ?) but the novel itself, a feminist blast of righteous anguish on the controversial theme of black men's violence against their women. In the form of letters from a barely literate black girl to her sister, Walker's novel had proved explosive, with a story of the rape and impregnation of a black girl by her father, then by her husband, and another narrative of a sexual relationship between two women.

Quincy Jones, who would compose the music, was a big fan of Spielberg and arranged a meeting with Alice Walker, who insisted on interviewing him before she would grant her approval for the adaptation of her novel. She had loved *E.T.* but would give the go-ahead only if she felt he had grasped the material. They got along beautifully. After all, though it was a story about incest, lesbianism, and domestic violence, it was above all—as Steven would be the first to understand—the story of a broken family.

Of all the influences that critics have noted on Spielberg and that he has himself acknowledged, perhaps the least talked about and most evident (next to John Ford) is *Gone with the Wind*, with its sweeping grandeur, its microcosm/macrocosm aesthetic, and its finger-in-every-pie producer David Selznick. After all, *The Color Purple*, like its predecessor, has a protracted and terrifying childbirth scene; it even has sex. But the major link is, of course, racial, the treatment of African Americans. Selznick, also a Jew who understood the history of prejudice, didn't want to go down in history as D. W. Griffith had, with the taint of having directed a racist masterpiece (*Birth of a Nation*). He wanted to "get it right" and did the best he could, given the time and place and the many conflicting voices hammering at him. But because those times were what they were, *Gone with the Wind* and its glorification of the southern planters as noble losers carried its racist legacy into the modern era. Nor would Spielberg altogether avoid similar blame. There would be the usual charges: He didn't understand blacks. He sentimentalized them, didn't show the poverty, and so on. (In fact, the family in *The Color Purple* is comparatively upscale, being property owners, but this didn't fit the stereotype.) Spielberg—also like Selznick preparing *Gone with the Wind*—was subjected to organized protests from black groups before he stepped onto the set. These continued and proliferated after the film's release, some feminists complained that the love scene between the two women wasn't explicit enough, and negative audience response was compounded by blistering attacks from critics.

The film's virtues got overlooked, among them the giant risk of casting not one but two novices—Whoopi Goldberg and Oprah Winfrey—in their first film roles. Whoopi was getting attention for her one-woman show, in which she impersonated a whole roster of characters. Asked to audition for Spielberg, she arrived at his private screening room to find herself confronted not just by the director but by luminaries like Alice Walker and Michael Jackson. It went so well that, as an encore, she performed her affectionate parody of E.T., an X-rated sendup in which the alien lands not in suburbia but in the hood, takes a turn as a pimp with earthling ho's, tries to call home from a pay phone that doesn't work. Though in private he laughed louder than anyone, the for-the-record Spielberg, when the story broke in the press, felt called upon to deplore the sight of E.T. with a coke spoon in his mouth.

Goldberg would have liked to play the defiant Sofia but was cast instead as Celie. Initially terrified, she was coached by Spielberg into giving a marvelously complex interpretation of the shy farm girl who gradually comes into her own. As for Oprah, it was Quincy Jones, visiting Chicago and watching television in his hotel room, who spotted her hosting a local talk show and immediately saw her as the fierce and physically imposing Sofia. Although Goldberg was intimidated by Oprah's apparent confidence, the local television personality also felt terribly insecure, stepping from small screen to large, and with a big-time director. Steven decided to forgo storyboards and leave room for improvisation; he spent hours guiding and reassuring the two women.

If Goldberg couldn't translate Celie's epistolary voice onto film, she beautifully renders her evolution from shy girl into confident woman, an awakening for which the alluring yet nurturing singer Shug (the beautiful Margaret Avery) is catalyst. Their love scene together, far from being the timid evasion criticized by many (including Walker and Spielberg himself, who later felt compelled to apologize for softening the sexuality), is filled with playful desire, all the more erotic for its relative reserve. The lovemaking may have been reduced to a kiss so as to avoid an R rating, or because of Spielberg's natural *pudeur*, but it's perfectly clear that the seduction by the worldly Shug of the timorous Celie is a physical, sexual relationship—indeed, may be the most sensual scene in all of Spielberg (a narrow field, to be sure)—playing out with the quiet confidence of a felt fantasy. In a typical Oscar absurdity *The Color Purple* gained eleven nominations: for best picture, all three actresses, screenplay, cinematography, and others, but none for Spielberg's direction.

The more legitimate charge against the movie is its overblown mise-en-scène, in which subtlety is sacrificed for a Disneyesque palette and music, overbright colors, and forced lyricism. The director is once again bedeviled by his own virtuosity, an instinct for the panoramic in which a shot diverts attention from the characters and becomes its own reason for being. Ultimately, it was not the racism but the grandiosity of the *Gone with the Wind* influence that threatened to capsize the film.

It had one eloquent defender in stormy-petrel film critic Armond White, who called it the best movie of 1985, suggesting that Spielberg approached it out of his own childlike perspective, bringing out "the feminist fairy tale essence of Walker's novel" through "his own pop-culture syntheses." White, who is African American, actually sees the movie's preoccupation with the oppression of women as a welcome relief from the kneejerk issue of racial discrimination. He concludes in a crescendo of Kaelish prose, "*The Color Purple* feels like the first insider's movie about Black America because the characters aren't defined by their relations to the white world nor created through a white artist's sympathetic condescension. These are new Black archetypes; as fictional creations they are so free of political justification that the whole issue of 'correctness' is zapped."[14]

10

Empire of the Sun

SHANGHAI, ON THE EVE of Pearl Harbor. The camera tracks along a muddy river where wreaths of flowers and wooden coffins are carried along by the tide like so much flotsam. The bow of a skiff ploughs heedlessly through the "debris." The camera pans to a church in the English quarter, where Chinese chauffeurs wax block-long Rolls-Royces and the exquisite strains of a boys choir rise overhead; inside, a boy's voice—a boy we soon know as Jamie—soars in a solo. After the service, we accompany Jamie to his walled-in mansion in the elegant English compound, and as he enters, the boy stares out the window at a grizzled beggar seated at his gate. The camera continues to chart the coexistence of two cultures, a desperate Chinese population of servants and refugees about to be invaded by the Japanese, and a hundred-year-old British community on the eve of flight or extinction. Motion and emotion have rarely been so expressively joined. Other Spielberg beginnings may be more dazzling, but this one, troubling and beautiful, haunts like a dream of one's own. The gliding movement of camera and limousine, the hushed interior, the shouts and threats of desperate refugees in the streets: this time the boy is on the inside looking out, but it's an inside that is no longer safe.

Another Spielberg movie centered on a child, but a movie, and a child, like no other. *Empire of the Sun* is the film in which a boy's fantasy of war as aerial glory crash-lands into reality, and overnight he finds himself alone, in a world shorn of all safeguards and security, where he will turn feral in order to survive. It is, in a strong if minority opinion (mine included), Spielberg's greatest film. Adapted from J. G. Ballard's semiautobiographical novel, it describes the author's own adventures as an English child cut adrift from his parents in the great Shanghai evacuation.

David Lean was originally slated to make the film, but he felt the shooting in China would be too strenuous, and in his view the story didn't have dramatic shape. Spielberg had planned to produce, but when he read the screenplay by Tom Stoppard, he longed to make it himself. Spielberg was immediately attracted to the idea of an adult world as seen through a child's point of view. It was, he said, the opposite of what had become his "credo: a man discovering things through the child in him."[1]

On the page it would seem to be a mismatch: Spielberg the optimist and humanist against one of the bleakest visions in contemporary fiction. J. G. Ballard would embrace, in science fiction, a kind of erotics of violence, his profoundly disillusioned view of humanity stemming from childhood exposure to war and atrocities that are virtually unimaginable, and certainly a stretch for a director who by his own admission had never seen a dead body or suffered real loss. Yet there are dozens of common points, primarily his innate affinity with

Innocence lost: an excited Jim (Christian Bale) is borne aloft during the evacuation of Shanghai in *Empire of the Sun*. Warner Bros./Photofest

childhood and children, along with his boy's love of planes (to the point that by his own admission they are practically a fetish in his movies), and perhaps more particularly a temperamental kinship with this driven little fellow, played magnificently by Christian Bale.

Spielberg discovered thirteen-year-old Bale through Amy Irving, who'd worked with him in a television movie. With Spielberg's sharp, sensitive handling, he gives one of the great child performances, going from a choirboy of seven or eight in a school blazer at the film's beginning, to the teenage war rat "Jim," living by his wits, old beyond his years, everything changed but his voice. The zest for war is alive in every fiber of his being, a reminder of feelings sublimated in adult men and rarely acknowledged in the antiwar theme of most war films—which, I think, more than the narrative problems to which Lean objected, accounts for the film's failure to garner a large audience. Viewers may have been uncomfortable with the terrible and exhilarating awakening of a child who welcomes the war with open arms.

Precocious, curious, spoiled, Jamie lives with his parents in the elite, British-dominated International Community under an uneasy peace. With his parents distracted, the boy cycles without permission through the raffish and dangerous streets of Shanghai, populated by gangs of beggars and kidnappers, and flies his balsa plane through battlefields strewn with unclaimed peasant bodies. In one of the most startling scenes, he comes upon the abandoned plane of a Japanese flier who has been shot down. He immediately climbs in, and begins playing with the controls, the child's admiration for Japanese skill and stoicism feeding an identification that will be one of the spiritual touchstones of his life.

For him, war, when it finally arrives in the form of the attack on the Chinese battleship *Petrel*, is a kind of welcome culmination, a clarifier, a holiday. Like the schoolboys in English director John Boorman's *Hope and Glory*, who after a nearby explosion, look to the skies and say "Thank you, Adolph," Jim, too, looks at the skies and gives thanks. In grappling directly with the nightmare of war—with mass evacuation, with forced labor camps, with divided loyalties and the bitter struggle to survive—the director prepares the way for *Schindler's List.* The theme of the broken family is his specialty, but now it can be broadened to other worlds and upheavals. From the English enclaves to the ghettoes, the rounding up of citizens, the forced transports that separated husbands from wives and parents from children, are prologue to the Holocaust.

Shanghai had peculiar personal resonance as well: relatives on his father's side had fled persecution in Russia and settled first in northern China, then in the Jewish section of the British protectorate, where they survived the war.

On the fateful day in December of 1941, there are rumors of a wider war in the Pacific, and the English have fled their gated mansions for presumed safety at a hotel in the Bund. That night, the Japanese bomb the *Petrel*, shattering the hotel's glass windows. The ever-wakeful Jamie has been standing at one of them, watching the action from afar, and using his flashlight to respond in semaphore to the signals at sea. When the explosion comes, he thinks he has started the war!

All is chaos as panicked throngs of English and Chinese and Eurasians flood the narrow avenue. In a stunningly choreographed scene of frenzy, the father disappears as Jamie and his mother are borne along on a tidal wave of fleeing humanity. From its soaring vantage point, the camera zooms in on the boy. In a split second, he must choose between the model plane, wrenched from one hand, and his mother, torn from the other. He runs after the plane.

Alone, he returns, as his mother has instructed, to the mansion on Amherst Avenue, now empty and in disarray, but with signs of struggle in his mother's bedroom. He hunkers down, stays for days, eating his way through the larder, watching as the water in the pool goes down and it fills with leaves, then snow. In a search for food, the boy, now an urchin but still wearing his prep school blazer, eventually hooks up with an unscrupulous American sailor named Basie (John Malkovich) and his louche cohorts. They are captured by Japanese troops and taken to the Lunghua detention center, where the already manic boy goes into overdrive, becoming a sort of middleman, racing between one faction and another, trading goods, learning to play the odds, to hustle and to depend on no one for his survival.

Basie is the roguish, charismatic surrogate father who contrasts with the upright responsible one in a split that will increasingly define Spielberg's twin poles of masculinity. Jamie, rechristened Jim by Basie, bonds instinctively with the Americans. In the prison camp, his one pal, as alien as E.T., is a Japanese youth on the other side of the divide, a kid who has his own toy plane and yearns to be a pilot. He ends up saving Jim's life, and losing his own, and Jim's terrible grief over him is part of *Empire of the Sun*'s great final act. The glorious Welsh lullaby Sua Gân, sung by the all-boy choir (and by Jim as soloist), that began the film now recurs when Jim salutes the Japanese pilots in their moment of surrender, one of the most moving sequences in all of Spielberg.

In another sign of redeemer humanity, an amoral, hollowed-out boy has somehow found his way out of mere selfish survival into compassion, maybe to some kind of God. He has refused to leave Mrs. Victor (Miranda Richardson) as she lies dying in the stadium to which they have been moved after the bombing of the camp. By daybreak, everyone else has gone, and as he clasps the dead woman's hand, Jim sees a bright light in the sky, which he believes is her soul floating to heaven. He later finds out it was the flash from the atomic bombing of Nagasaki, hundreds of miles away. Thus Spielberg, perhaps unique among directors, manages to capture both the terrible import of this image and its otherworldly beauty as well.

The reunion with his parents, who at first don't recognize him nor he them, pierces the heart for all that is left unsaid. For so long, Jim has acted out of compulsion, racing against time as if to pause might be to die. Or might make him vulnerable to the tug of a past that seems impossibly far away and parents whose faces he can no longer remember. Now we look over his mother's shoulder at his troubled yet dazed eyes. He has seen things they will never see, learned things that forever separate him from them. He has gone past them, in ways that children do, but because of the accelerated effect of war, more irrevocably, and more wrenchingly.

In an image both richly reverberant yet going beyond the director's previous work, it's what E.T. might have felt if we had followed him to his planet—he'd finally gotten home, only to realize he no longer fit in. That ultimate isolation—the loneliness of growing up and beyond one's parents, has its most potent expression here. Nothing is force-fed, nothing underlined. *Empire* ends not with reassurance but with a question mark. What will this boy become?

At this time, Spielberg, another boy-man possessed of an overactive metabolism, was behaving, as one associate put it, like a man who'd drunk four cups of coffee; having—in Kathleen Kennedy's words—"an idea every thirteen seconds."[2] And although he had been true to his vow to take more time off to be with the adored Max, his compulsion to work took the form of producing a number of films with other directors, many ill-advised, while amassing an empire of his own. He was acquiring a mogul-like taste for the perks of the elite—art, planes, multiple homes—under the expert tutelage of Steve Ross.

Tutorials included trips to Acapulco on Big Steve's plane, where Steven would wake in the night with movie ideas. Like many middle-of-the-night ideas, some were good, but most seemed to wind up in the hands of other directors under his production banner. With mentor-mogul largesse he was throwing money at protégé directors and paying fatally little attention to scripts. There would be a few successes (*Back to the Future*, *Who Framed Roger Rabbit*) and many flops (*The Goonies*, *The Money Pit*, *Joe versus the Volcano*, *The Flintstones*), all based on some fleeting childhood experience, fear, idea. They simply had to be made, as if some moment of his childhood, some wisp of a story heard sitting on his father or grandfather's knee, would slip away forever.

Also, sadly but perhaps inevitably, he had become isolated by his success. As his friend Bob Gale pointed out, he was a little like Jamie in *Empire of the Sun*. He lived in Hollywood's version of the British settlement, encased in a cushy, opulent environment where he was privileged but lonely. And, Gale might have added, his Basie was the dubious Steve Ross.

Spielberg wasn't someone who enjoyed success for its own sake, and being a mogul must have felt less real than movies, to which he connected in such a visceral way. His imaginative field of vision was like Ballard's in its blurring of real and fictional worlds, in its sense of images dominating reality. A poster of *Gone with the Wind* appears, in both movie and book, amid the chaos of the bombing. David Selznick intrudes his presence upon Spielberg once again, as, in a crowded Shanghai street, the gigantic image of Clark Gable and Vivien Leigh embracing against the flames of Atlanta towers above the movie palace in the Bund, just as smoke—as if from those very fires—fills the Chinese sky. As one war merges into another, it's as if the movie poster comes to claim the higher reality, flattening out the "real" world into its own two-dimensional image.

11

Indiana Jones and the Last Crusade, Always, and Hook

Spielberg needed a break after two strenuously ambitious grown-up films, so it was back to the sandbox with George Lucas for another outing with Indy. But first there was a birthday to celebrate. With becoming modesty, Spielberg had distanced himself from a comparison with Orson Welles—though it was he who brought it up in the first place, but no such disclaimers were forthcoming regarding *Citizen Kane.* He had even bought the Rosebud sled: it was his prize collectible. So Amy Irving rounded up friends and clips to make a video, *Citizen Spielberg,* to be shown in 1987 on his fortieth birthday. (Actually his forty-first, but the competitive date-fudging hadn't been exposed.) In a parody of the March of Time format, complete with orotund narrator (Dan Aykroyd), we are invited to ogle and admire the costly pleasure dome that is Amblin, the "world's largest Taco Bell," in the heart of Universal Studios, with fifteen thousand video games, and a natural zoo "complete with beast of the field and fowl of the air." The movie includes friends and family (with footage of Spielberg's parents before he was born), interviews with a sister, and, from Arizona, the maid and the family hairdresser. Little Max says "Daddy, I love you," Barbra Streisand sings Happy Birthday à la Marilyn Monroe, and a U-Haul carrying Steve's own version of Rosebud concludes the film.

Amblin was grandiose, yes; but there was nothing derelict about Universal's monument to its star talent. Nor was there much resemblance between the two cinemagicians, Spielberg the endlessly youthful Prince Hal, always in touch with his audience, Welles, the Falstaffian genius cast off by Hollywood well before his fortieth birthday. The longevity battle was no contest.

Still, time was marching on even for Spielberg. *Indiana Jones and the Last Crusade* allowed the director to "consciously regress" once again, but with a Holy Grail straight from the analyst's couch: a reconciliation between father and son in the irresistible duo of crusty scholar Indy Senior (Sean Connery) and Harrison Ford as swashbuckling son with daddy issues.[1]

Most reviewers found it mechanical, a falling off in energy, none of which deterred the ever-growing fan base. The films had always been critic-proof, but this proved to be Spielberg's biggest hit since *E.T.*, making $474.7 million worldwide, having cost only 44 million. And—his "best memory from the entire year"—he was honored by the Boy Scouts of America with the Distinguished Eagle Scout Award.

One shouldn't underestimate the importance of even the lesser of the Indiana Jones films in Spielberg's artistic development. Complicated and with different rhythmic and architectural challenges, the action-packed pyrotechnics allowed him to experiment with craft—he always said he learned more from them than from the more serious and personal ones. With its bright flat colors and exaggerated thrills and spills, *The Last*

Crusade continues the cartoon tradition established by *Raiders*, but as is customary, Spielberg weaves through the bold genre graphics his own personal themes. You didn't need to decipher a Rorschach test to see the father-son relationship emerge front and center.

We begin with a Wild West backstory situating Indy as a Boy Scout in Utah in 1912. He returns home breathless, having eluded rapacious thieves, a close encounter that goes unobserved by the scholar hunched over an ancient manuscript—his father. Though we don't see his face until halfway through the movie, Connery's Professor Henry Jones invigorates the story, providing a moral compass—sort of. An ornery cuss, but, unlike his more materialistic son, a true believer, he's obsessed with finding the Holy Grail for its own sake rather than any profits that might accrue. Originally Jones Sr. was to appear only at the end, but happily, he occupies more space, becoming the fulcrum of Indy's own search for identity. Whether this was Spielberg's idea, or Lucas's, or screenwriter Jeffrey Boam's, or, as seems apparent from various reports, a felicitous amalgam, it was Spielberg who insisted that Sean Connery play Indy's father over Lucas's vision of him as a sexless fuddy-duddy. And here we might pause to consider another cojones-enhancing decision of Spielberg's: it was he who insisted on the surname Jones over Lucas's original Indiana Smith!

The Indy series was originally meant to rival the Bond films and go one better. Even Alison Doody, the actress/model who played the Nazi-sympathizing archeologist Elsa, was a Bond babe. She was also the least interesting love interest yet, more dominatrix than playmate; her scenes with Ford, meant to be screwball witty ("I don't like forward women" says Indy; "I hate arrogant men," says Elsa), are merely facetious, their embraces a parody of ravenous lust. The eyebrow-raising kicker was the revelation that father and son had shared her favors. The two Indys sleeping with the same woman? Here was a literalization of the Oedipal conceit of *Back to the Future*—a tad too literal for Steven, apparently, who wanted it out. The director may have officially objected to the off-color triangle, but it speaks to that occasional eruption of sneaky X-rated humor. Whatever the reservations, Connery, relishing the raunchy and unpaternal aspects of the character, prevailed.

The theme of coming to understand and reconcile with the father was in the forefront of the director's imagination. He and Arnold had been estranged for years: Steven's casual attitude to college, and their arguments over the boy's future, had hardened into a permanent divide. But once Steven had a child, they entered into a different relationship, two fathers, two workaholic fathers at that. Steven was ready to loosen up and have fun with the new perspective of seeing fatherhood from both points of view. Rather than wanting to "cut to the chase," he was willing to practically cut out the chase, or at least dawdle in the father-son duets, which, as in so many buddy films of the period, sparkle with the love-hate odd-couple dynamic missing in the boy-girl plot. Indy flails around, vanquishing bad guys, in what we imagine as a recapitulation of his, and young Steven's, childhood behavior, consistently trying and failing to get his father's attention. After one more death-defying feat in which the son has saved the unappreciative father's life, they are relaxing in a bar, and Indy tries to lay a guilt trip on Dad, complaining that when he was growing up his father took no notice of him. Connery jauntily replies that he wasn't worth noticing till he grew up, and then he went away and it was too late.

Elsa, harsh and facetious, sometimes ally, sometimes enemy, seems there to illustrate the treachery of women, and, ironically, to serve as a catalyst for bringing father and son together. Talk about finessing the Oedipal contest. First they share her, then they share the joke of having shared her. Their bond consolidated, they ride off into the sunset together at the film's end, leaving Elsa, destroyed by her own greed, disintegrating in the dust.

And in another stroke of life and art intertwining, it was Kate Capshaw, Spielberg's next ladylove, who would persuade him to reconcile with his father. Even as Spielberg was recovering from the failed relationship with Amy, Kate and Steven were spending time together. Fittingly, she would even fly to London in 1989 for the premiere of *Last Crusade*, a film celebrating the reconciliation of father and son.

Of course, the Lucas-Spielberg films are a mash-up of pop cultural, mythical, and religious motifs and archetypes, with Lucas more into Jungian figurations and Steven of a more mystical bent. We're not meant to take these sacred totems too seriously, any more than we're to take offense at the pop-up villains drawn from Third World populations. But reviewers did take offense. After charges of racism, *The Last Crusade* skirts the problem with safely demonized Nazis and some brown-skinned villains of indeterminate ethnicity. In a more diverse and globally aware world, ruled by political correctness and terrified of offending minorities (now majorities), it was becoming harder and harder to find safely despicable "Others"; generally the Nazis were the only available villains whose dignity and inner lives didn't need to be considered. But where Lucas and Spielberg get into trouble is in the gap between content and execution—between the pulpy material . . . and the extreme sophistication of the storytelling. Spielberg's skill at humanizing his characters just enough to draw one in, primarily through the universal nexus of family and childhood, creates a felt reality in which the two-dimensional characters seem out of place.

Spielberg's recognition of himself in his workaholic father represented a major shift in sympathy, and it was a theme that would play out in *Hook*, Spielberg's Peter Pan movie, two years later. In both films, as in *Empire of the Sun*, there would be surrogate father figures: in *Last Crusade* it is the handsome head honcho of the gang of thieves, who recognizes little Indy's bravery and gives him the fedora that will become his trademark. And there would be a newly rueful view of childhood from the parents' point of view.

But in between there was a major rupture, which would also make its way into a film. Divorce. Amy could no longer endure the burdens and disadvantages that went with being Spielberg's wife. Their many houses and the grandiose lifestyle favored by her mogul husband were alien to her simpler tastes, and her career seemed stalled in a no-win conundrum: She couldn't play in his films for fear of charges of nepotism. And other directors were loath to hire her because nobody wanted to risk working with Spielberg's wife and have him looking over their shoulders. The one exception was a woman director, Joan Micklin Silver, who starred Amy in *Crossing Delancey* and told me that Steven came to the set several times and offered a grinning thumbs-up of support.

Custody arrangements were made, and Irving received a monumental settlement. The terms were never disclosed, but assuming she was awarded half his worth, estimates of her windfall ranged from $93 million to $112.5 million. The parting seemed amicable, with both parents determined to make life as secure as possible for Max, and so agreeing that one of them would always stay with him when the other was away working.

The movie that reflected the rupture and the permanence of loss was the romantic ghost drama *Always*, Spielberg's remake of Victor Fleming's World War II classic *A Guy Named Joe*, with Spencer Tracy and Irene Dunne. Would this be the woman's picture he had claimed to want to make? The director had seen the 1943 movie in Phoenix as his parents' marriage was coming apart, and he claimed it was the second movie, after *Bambi*, that made him cry. And well it might. Tracy gives one of his most moving performances as the flier who, after fatally crashing, is allowed to return from the afterlife to witness his bereaved ladylove as she begins making a life for herself. Dunne is also powerfully affecting as she gradually falls in love with another man under the gaze of her invisible husband. Spielberg transplants the action to civilian firefighters in present-day Montana, with Richard Dreyfuss as Pete, the doomed aviator, and Holly Hunter as Dorinda, his fiancée, a dispatcher with flying ambitions of her own. When the story is taken out of its war setting, we lose the sense of urgency and self-sacrifice that was quintessential in those forties films. A volunteer brigade of men fighting brushfires, even at great personal risk, doesn't rise to the level of heroism that was automatically conferred on our men in uniform.

Even more important, the romance isn't romantic. Hunter is scrappy, funny, argumentative, and pure tomboy, more like a playmate or a sister. Even her professional ambition has a kind of wistful, aw-shucks-I'm-just-a-girl quality. The movie that *Always* more closely resembles is Howard Hawks's classic flier-cum-love story *Only Angels Have Wings*, starring Cary Grant as the head of a group of mail-carrying pilots flying dangerous routes through the Andes, and Jean Arthur as the down-on-her-luck entertainer who lands in their South American port and falls in love with him. It shares with *Always* the same buddy angle (John Goodman playing to Dreyfuss the role Thomas Mitchell served with Grant), and a girl who can hang out at a bar as "one of the guys," trading banter in screwball style.

And then there is the captivating love story between Cary Grant and Jean Arthur. Both Arthur and Hunter have the familiar and often wince-making female task of trying to stop the man from "doing what a man's gotta do," in this case flying. But Arthur's essential femininity, her allure, is never in doubt. It goes without saying.

Holly Hunter's, on the other hand, must be said. At her

birthday party, a feminization occurs. She descends the steps in a bar full of gaping men, wearing a white gown ("girly clothes"), a scene that recalls the similar transformation of Karen Allen in *Raiders of the Lost Ark*, when the tomboy emerges in a dress, looking like a little girl in mommy's clothes.

Spielberg's shortcomings in portraying adult men and women are painfully on view. The antierotic, overgrown kid quality is inscribed in the casting. Dreyfuss and Hunter can do romantic comedy, but erotic yearning is beyond them. The drawback is not, as many have charged, that Spielberg can't "do sex." He can't (the couple's one scene in bed is like a sleepover), but so what? Many, even most, directors can't, and shouldn't even try. Spielberg's problem is wider and deeper: he can't imagine the full spectrum of adult heterosexual emotions—attraction, flirtation, desire, even good conversation between a man and a woman. He may have loved old Hollywood movies, but was deaf and blind to the language of love at their core, the visual and verbal, the eros of the "look."

The one truly heartrending love scene in *Always* is about absence and loss: Dorinda is dancing to "their" song "Smoke Gets in Your Eyes," while Pete dances alongside her, unseen. He says "Sleep tight, baby sister," and we feel real love here, if more sibling than sensual, as if by giving up his role as erotic lover, he is free to express a different, more familial and—in the Spielberg hierarchy—stronger emotion.

A corollary of this blind spot, this failure to pass through Oedipal conflict and come out the other side, is Spielberg's inability to portray rivalry between men of roughly equal status: the neophyte flier played by Brad Johnson (vs. Van Johnson in the original) is a doofus. Pete is supposed to resent but gradually accept the young flier who is replacing him, eventually serving as his mentor. The mentor role is one Spielberg has relished, as long as—in most cases—the protégé poses no real threat to his own preeminence.

In an odd if rather charming twist on the original, Spielberg turns the cameo part of God—Lionel Barrymore in the earlier film—into a spirit-woman played by Audrey Hepburn. In her last film role the waif who was always the most tomboyish of actresses mutates into a quasi-maternal guardian angel.

A critical and commercial failure, *Always* is one of Spielberg's most awkward movies, yet there are moments of magic: breathtaking flying sequences and the sublime dance scene. Holly Hunter in her solitude makes us understand what it feels to have loved, and to be utterly alone. If Spielberg's heart isn't "into" romance or desire, the emotion of longing is one he deeply understands.

In *Hook*, the noisy mechanical Spielberg is at the helm, the sweet side only intermittently apparent. This is his 1991 version of *Peter Pan*, starring Robin Williams as a corporate workaholic who needs to get in touch with his inner child in order to man up and recapture the love of his son.

In the early eighties, Spielberg had planned to make a singing and dancing version for Disney, using the original J. M. Barrie story and starring Michael Jackson in the lead—an audaciously interesting idea, which might have been just the right version at the right time. But Max had recently arrived, and Spielberg didn't want to take time off from fatherhood to go to London. So a decade later he makes a film about a father traveling to London who is too busy to pay attention to his son. Peter Banning, glued to his cell phone, a corporate arbitrageur ("I missed the sixties because I was an accountant"—suggests a sly dig at Spielberg's own nose-to-the-grindstone stint in television during the acid-dropping years), has promised and failed to attend his son's ballgame one too many times and risks losing Jackie's love. On a Christmas (!) trip to London to visit Grandma Wendy (Maggie Smith), Jackie and his sister Maggie are kidnapped by the minions of Captain Hook (Dustin Hoffman). With the help of Tinkerbell (Julia Roberts), Peter must return to Neverland to recapture his childhood memories and his flying skills, and thereby rescue his children in a final showdown with Hook.

If *Last Crusade* was an act of "regression," *Hook* is a film *about* regression, meant to utilize the insights into his own infantilism that the director had gleaned from the analyst's couch. Perhaps because Spielberg had his analyst—John Bradshaw, shrink to the stars—as an adviser on the set, or because of where he was in his life, *Hook* was less an exorcism than a show-and-tell in which all his signature themes trot out, take a frantic bow, and retreat, more in desperation than resolution.

In a two-part *Film Comment* article in 1992, critic Henry Sheehan wrote perceptively that "every Spielberg hero from *Duel* onward is, to one extent or another, worried that he is failing at some essentially male role, either lover or father. In *Hook* these twin fears are merged in Peter, who is plainly a poor father and who, less conspicuously, wants to retreat from the issue of sex in general."[2]

The idea reportedly originated with screenwriter Jim V. Hart's three-year-old son, who asked his dad what would happen if Peter Pan grew up . . . and if Hook was not dead. But *Hook* wrenches *Peter Pan* from its context—the context of all fairy tales—of being frozen in time. The eternal boy, beardless and sensitive, inhabits the charmed world of the nursery, a place of imagination, dedicated to the avoidance of adult masculinity. "I don't ever want to be a man, yuk!" says the child actor in the school play that begins the film, and Grandma Wendy forbids everyone in her house to grow at all. In the kinky gender dynamics of the play, Peter is generally played by a girl, a "trans" or asexual choice that serves two purposes: the actor/character can take on sensitive qualities that would be "sissy" if possessed by a boy, and she can never grow up to be a man.

Spielberg was wrestling with the conundrum: how to keep

the uninhibited freedom of the child's imagination and still grow into an adult? But his inner compass, his sense of himself in the world, was shifting, and the man who had made *Empire of the Sun* could no longer fully believe in childhood innocence.

He had become a workaholic—the very thing he hated in his father—and was afflicted with that obsession of baby boomer parents, the conflict between family and career. *Hook*, as if infected by this desperate ambivalence—critic J. Hoberman called it "Peter Panic"—went way over budget and never found its way between the literal and the ethereal.[3] A fine, skeptical Charlie Korsmo, as Jackie, is one of Spielberg's least starry-eyed kids. Likewise, Julia Roberts's incorporeal Tinker Bell is given grown-up feelings, an earthly yen that the uncarnal Peter can't reciprocate. Located in some strange limbo between childhood and adulthood, the fairy dust doesn't ignite, but adulthood seems to offer all the pleasures of a life sentence. Witness a startlingly subversive riff on the joylessness of parenthood. The setting is the schoolroom, and the professor, the bad-fun father Hook, asks Maggie why she and Jack think their parents love them.

"Mommy reads to us every night because she loves us," says the girl. "No!" Hook rasps, "to stupefy you to sleep so she and Daddy can sit down for three measly minutes without your extremely irritating and repetitious 'I want a cookie, I want a pottie, I want I want, me, me, me, mine mine mine now now now!' . . . They were happier and freer before you were born."

Also funny, utilizing the glorious fast-talking skills of Williams, another Spielberg surrogate, is the verbal swordplay between Peter and the Lost Boys, a smutty rapid-fire duel of real and made-up dirty words. It's hard to know just who composed these symphonies of invective. As usual, there were many cooks contributing their screenwriting skills, perhaps even more than usual. Carrie Fisher was one. Jim Hart, *Hook*'s credited screenwriter, said Spielberg "tended to use writers like paintbrushes."[4]

His brain was a magnet for ideas. According to those around him, when he got excited by one, he wound up feeling like it was his own.

To add to the man's frenzy, he was still caught emotionally between two women. His marriage with Amy had ended, but he was slow in announcing the divorce, and also reluctant to acknowledge his increasingly serious affair with Capshaw, even though they'd had a baby by this time. (Amy had meanwhile taken up with Brazilian filmmaker Bruno Barreto, whom she would marry in 1996.) Whatever the obstacles, though, Kate's campaign was paying off. They were living together, and she would come to the premiere of *Hook* in London.

While waiting for his divorce to come through, she cared for an African foster baby, Theo, whom the couple would later adopt. In 1990 she gave birth to Sasha, a girl and her first child with Spielberg. Around the same time, she converted from Methodism to Judaism—a move many thought calculated to snare the born-again director, but which seems to have been genuinely felt. She told an interviewer that she was drawn to the faith because of its emphasis on family, and she seemed to actively encourage Steven in his embrace of Judaism and philanthropy. She was family-oriented (that "familiar scent"), and with her dual identities, shiksa and Jew, Steven got to have his cake and eat it too. The couple would marry in 1992 in East Hampton and eventually have houses there and in Pacific Palisades to take care of their expanding family. On Long Island's East End, he came to be known as both benefactor and beneficiary, supporter of causes as well as indulger in some well-deserved fun. Among the bequests was the Southampton Hospital's Kate Capshaw and Steven Spielberg Fast Track Nursing Station. On the luxury end of the fast-track spectrum, there were horses for the children and private planes and a 282-foot yacht docked in Florida and dinner parties on the beach near his Georgica estate, complete with servants and table linens.

Weekly renters would seem to have enjoyed the yacht more than Spielberg. The ever-hyper mogul not only needed to be working constantly, but he needed to satisfy the different parts of himself by tackling different kinds of projects simultaneously. He adhered to a division reminiscent of Graham Greene's between "entertainment" and "literature"; in Spielberg's case, the work split between adventure/fantasy "flicks" and serious "films." As with Greene, however, Spielberg's divisions were never airtight, and the "entertainments" were often superior to the "important" films.

A more reliable division in Spielberg's oeuvre is between the winningly benevolent take on the world in his signature films, and a warped and subversive perspective in the films he produced. But even his own films were becoming increasingly chiaroscuro, blending light and shadow. At the same time, he was as incapable of forgoing the instincts of a showman as he was of skirting what he saw as his responsibilities as a teacher and moralist.

12

Schindler's List, Jurassic Park, *and the Shoah Foundation*

We are now in Płaszów, Poland, in the winter of 1993, and in frigid temperatures under lowering skies, Jews are herded through the streets or gunned down like animals in the 1943 liquidation of the ghetto. After shooting such scenes, Spielberg comes home to his rented house, where, surrounded by Kate and his children, he weeps. The film has opened a floodgate of memories and stories, hitherto repressed, of relatives who suffered or died in the camps. For solace, he has his brood of children. There are five now, Max, Sasha, and Sawyer (a son born 1992), their adopted Theo, and Jessica, Kate's daughter from her previous marriage. They talk about *Jurassic Park*, and comic relief is provided by his pal Robin Williams, who calls him periodically with "CARE packages," impromptu monologues that were dependably hilarious.

Yet for all its promise of fun for the kids, *Jurassic Park* wasn't just a tame outing at the petting zoo. It was more of a *Jaws* of the Jungle, with children as dinosaur prey, and got a PG-13 rating because of it. The theme of children at risk crops up in a startlingly high percentage of his films, and reaches a fine climax when Tyrannosaurus rex chomps on a car with the kiddies inside. Spielberg delighted in testing the limits of acceptable violence, playing sadistic games with his teenage audience. Like many kids, Spielberg had been fascinated with dinosaurs since he was a child, often visiting the local natural history museum, and he knew as soon as he read the galleys of Michael Crichton's novel that he wanted to make the movie. Both book and movie employed a canny mix of action-adventure and pseudoscience gobbledygook about the cloning of dinosaurs from prehistoric DNA. Screenwriters David Koepp and Crichton, with help from Malia Scotch Marmo, attempted to introduce tensions between characters who were razor-thin as written.

Richard Attenborough plays John Hammond, the impresario of the park, host to paleontologist guests with relationship issues: the gloomy Alan (Sam Neill) and his grad student and would-be spouse, the fearful Ellie (Laura Dern). The little ones—Hammond's two grandchildren—are prime dinosaur fodder. Introducing an infantophobe theme not in the novel, Neill's character loathes the kids, rebuffing the boy's worshipful overtures, growling at him, refusing even to ride in the same Jeep with him. Does real-life superdad of four harbor the occasional subversive wish to make them disappear? Or possibly Alan's chilly indifference is the residual bad-dad reflex attached to Arnold. Ultimately, this is a fairy tale from the Good Steven with a happy ending, as the kids and their surrogate parents unite, and father and surrogate son bond.

But the dinosaurs were always going to be the main attraction, with the lumbering Tyrannosaurus rex, her head rising quizzically over the landscape, vying for the role of hero with the sleeker, more "modern" velociraptor—both more "real" than the flesh-and-blood characters.

Spielberg saw them as individuals, spending hours storyboarding their moves, finding visual touches and noises to characterize each species. The director knew what he wanted before he knew how to get it, and what he eventually got was a technological revolution. Or at least a giant evolutionary step that would alter filmmaking.

Three-dimensional live-action figures created through computer-generated imagery (CGI), developed by Dennis Muren, represented a huge advance, not just over the stop-motion miniature techniques of Ray Harryhausen and other special-effects pioneers (think *King Kong*), but even over the go-motion techniques of Lucas's Industrial Light and Magic. Spielberg was convinced that CGI wasn't yet up to creating a full-size dinosaur. Muren disagreed. He came in one day with a test screening, and the director was stunned. So was production supervisor Jules Roman, who was forced to admit his own obsolescence in a line—"I think I'm extinct"—that Spielberg promptly inserted into the screenplay.[1] Delighted and bewildered by the new toy, Spielberg even took a crash course in computer technology, capitulating to the academic specialty—science—he'd always held against his father!

Stephen Jay Gould, always a canny guide at the intersection of pop culture and nerd science, praised the dinosaurs extravagantly, ridiculing intellectuals who couldn't appreciate the complexity of creating such an organism. But he chided Spielberg for marginalizing the most exciting part of the Crichton story, the crucial place given to chaos theory, in favor of the usual cautionary pablum about man's hubris.[2]

In its frightening verisimilitude, the movie becomes a kind of ur-parable on the technological evolution of filmmaking itself, a story of the decline and fall of human characters in the wake of cinema's relentless march away from film and toward animation. This had to be exciting to Spielberg, as evidenced by the course he took, but perhaps it was also a harbinger of a future he wasn't entirely comfortable with.

The movie itself, with its thrill rides and gift shop of prehistoric-style tchotchkes, was itself a dinosaur theme park, positioned to create its own unstoppable commercial momentum. Yet the director's trademark humanity is still on view, precisely in the scrappiness and disorder of the characters, the grounding in the nuclear family, that give his films a certain tension absent in many of the more formulaic action movies of his competitors.

There were other personal twists as well, such as the movie's remodeling of the character of Attenborough's Hammond. In the book he's pure con man or "carny" man—a stick figure of capitalist greed who'll do anything to make his park succeed (shades of the bad, Steven Ross–influenced Spielberg); in the film he has become a quasi-honorable showman, exonerated by his passion for introducing his pet project to the world.

The genial but morally enigmatic entertainer, the artist-showman with his stable of workers and performers who do his bidding: if Attenborough's parkmeister fits this description, so does Herr Direktor Oskar Schindler—and so does Herr Direktor Spielberg himself.

"I'm a presenter," says Liam Neeson's Oskar, extending his arms in a swashbuckling gesture of magnanimity, or self-delight. Spielberg, like Thomas Keneally, was drawn to the true story of the businessman-turned-rescuer-hero, not a Jew saving Jews but a *Nazi* saving Jews.

It was in 1982, reading a review of Keneally's *Schindler's List*, that Sid Sheinberg at Universal brought the book to Spielberg's attention. The director was sufficiently intrigued by the paradox of Schindler's nature that Universal bought the property

The humanity: Liam Neeson and Steven Spielberg on the set of *Schindler's List.* Universal/Photofest

for him. But it took ten years for events to persuade him to make the film. One "event" was the sheer persistence of Poldek Pfefferberg, a survivor whose family had been saved by Oskar Schindler, and who had originally pressed the industrialist's story on Keneally. He appears in the roll call of survivors who walk before the camera at the end of the film, and it would be to the Polish worker that Spielberg gave thanks when the movie won the Academy Award.

There were a number of screenplays; other directors, like Roman Polanski and Martin Scorsese, were close to signing on. One important influence on Spielberg was Billy Wilder. Most of the great director's family had been killed in Auschwitz, and Wilder felt passionately about the project. Like Kubrick, he had wanted to make such a film himself, and his emotional urgency infected Spielberg. Further incentive was provided by daily reports of the persecution of religious minorities and of "ethnic cleansing" in Bosnia.

Schindler: a man who was a sensualist, a gambler, a bon vivant, but above all a man driven to make money. That this industrialist and black-market profiteer would, in the early days of World War II, first hire Jews to work in his ceramics and munitions factory (they were cheaper), then become so obsessed with saving them that he would endanger his life to rescue eleven hundred Jews from Auschwitz, sabotage his own factory, and berate himself for not saving more, is a puzzle, a mystery of personal transformation, that lies at the core of both the book and the film. That Spielberg allows us to see and accept this metamorphosis without fully understanding it, is one of the signal virtues of the film.

The young man's need to discover and enshrine substitute fathers, seductive "fun" fathers, at the expense of "loser" dads found its real-life equivalent in his attachment to Steve Ross, now the Time Warner chairman, to whom *Schindler's List* is dedicated. He credited Ross with "opening my heart" to private philanthropy. According to most views, Spielberg's view of Ross was as much a fantasy as anything Frank Capra ever invented, the rogue as Santa Claus. The real professional godfather who persistently helped, guided, and watched out for Spielberg was Sid Sheinberg at Universal. Spielberg understood and appreciated Sheinberg's huge investment in his career, but he also needed to imagine a personal father figure who embodied Ross's flash and swagger.

Was Oskar similarly romanticized by Spielberg? Some who knew the Nazi's history protested that the full range of Oskar's duplicities and failings are not on view. The man had been in German intelligence and later would be a double agent. But dramatic compressions are necessary, and the movie implies enough of the man's moral and ethical laxity to confirm his transgressions.

Only Spielberg, as he himself candidly admitted, had the clout to get a Hollywood studio to back such a film, which not only dealt with a downbeat subject but promised to be brutally realistic by industry standards. In anticipation of uncertain commercial prospects and because he didn't want to accept "blood money," he gave up his salary, deferred his percentage of gross film rentals, and when the film actually went on to become a commercial success, donated the profits through his Righteous Persons Foundation to Jewish organizations, including the one he founded after making the film, the Survivors of the Shoah Visual History Foundation.

Schindler's List would be the most celebrated film of his career, hailed as a high-water mark signaling a new maturity, but it was also the most virulently attacked. He expected negative criticism, though perhaps not of such intensity. He knew he was walking a tightrope. Any movie on the Holocaust was going to be passionately scrutinized, especially, of course, by Jews, most of whom had been touched directly or indirectly by the horror. At one extreme were those who felt, with the philosopher

Theodor Adorno, that any attempt to describe the Holocaust in fiction or poetry was unacceptable, a sacrilege against the ungraspable enormity of the event. This would be especially true of a film, and a "Hollywood" film at that, which would inevitably aim for "entertainment," however subdued or restrained.

Even those who, with the passage of time, and the realization of the necessity to process and bear witness, no longer held to such a strict taboo were disturbed that an important movie about the Holocaust showed Jews being saved not by Jews but by a gentile. Or that it emphasized the few who were saved rather than the six million who died. Or that it didn't portray the Jews as "characters in their own right." It would seem that any work, particularly any film, that tries to deal with that vast and incomprehensible enormity of the twentieth century is almost doomed by definition to fall short.

Naturally, Spielberg—never a we-versus-them person—would be alert to the inherent drama of the situation; would wonder about the Nazis, often portrayed monolithically in lockstep (or goose step) as the embodiment of evil. Moreover, as someone long in hiding from his Jewish identity, Spielberg had studied and adapted to the gentiles around him and, in assimilating, had learned their ways. He felt kinship with Ben Kingsley's Itzhak Stern, the stubborn accountant who appeals to Oskar's better nature. He was also able to enter into the vile and tortured psyche of Amon Goeth, "Oskar's dark brother," as Keneally described him, and to find the occasional soft spot within the crazy overseer, so brilliantly played by Ralph Fiennes, who shoots Jews for target practice from his villa deck.

The physically imposing Neeson's height is emphasized, giving Oskar stature and a symbolic perspective. Detached from the proceedings, he is able to see farther than other people. This is brought home most vividly in the moment in which he sits astride a horse on the hill overlooking Kraków, his eyes—and ours—transfixed by the evacuation, culminating in the moment when the girl in the red dress darts across his field of vision. As controversial as any "issue" in the film was this boldly aestheticizing gesture—a red smear in the middle of a black-and-white film. Opinion divided. Was it a masterstroke or an instant visual cliché? Probably a little of both. But the theatricality of this gash in the film evokes not only a little girl's love of color (also in the book), but the other red, the red of blood. It underlines and "individualizes" the victimized Jews. The fancy series of shots—point and counterpoint—in a movie that resolutely avoids exhibitionism expresses a crucial connection between seeing and understanding: as those below are scurrying, their views restricted, Oskar becomes both witness and conscience.

The Polish cinematographer Janusz Kaminski, who would become Spielberg's trusted eyes for most of the rest of his career, followed the director's concept of direct, documentary-like storytelling, often using handheld camera, and filming in black and white to give the story a kind of newsreel immediacy.

One source of dispute between the director and screenwriter was that Steve Zaillian wanted to shape the film "vertically," through Oskar, with the industrialist appearing in virtually every scene, whereas Spielberg wanted to spread out "horizontally," inclusively. The director finds a judicious balance between individualizing the Jews—by introducing brief scenes in which they argue about what they should do; by showing a few faces that are etched on our memory—and also, realistically and symbolically, folding them into the blur of a nearly inhuman mass. As Primo Levi wrote in that greatest and most eloquent book *The Drowned and the Saved*, people lose their individuality as soon as they become oppressed, defined as a group.[3] That's why names are so important, as Spielberg and Zaillian understand: Jewish names, first typed in a list and called out for what we think is deportation, but is employment—names typed on Schindler's list and marked for salvation.

Crowned by many as a masterpiece, called his "bar mitzvah" by others, *Schindler* was nominated for twelve Oscars and won seven, including Best Picture and Best Director (Spielberg's first), Screenplay, Cinematography, and Score. Liam Neeson and Ralph Fiennes were nominated for Best Actor and Best Supporting Actor. There would be awards overseas, and intangible consequences, raising Spielberg to an international public figure. Perceptions of the character of the man and the nature of his gifts had now to be reassessed, a certain comfortable condescension jolted into something like respect.

Hollywood and the critics had pigeonholed him as an artistic lightweight so that even his mega-successes could be written off as inferior genre pieces, fantasy or action adventure "flicks" targeted at the adolescent audience. The wealth was absurd, but even more so was his shambolic self-presentation—the baseball cap, the messy-room look—which suggested a teenager home from college and determined to annoy his parents. Who could take him seriously?

The envy-tinged disdain had been replaced by schadenfraude at a string of failures. With *The Color Purple*, *Hook*, and *Empire of the Sun*, Hollywood settled into a collective smirk of gratification: obviously, he could only do one kind of film. Once Spielberg left his comfort zone for "grown-up" films with meaning, he was out of his depth—in his own words, "wearing the wrong shoe size."[4] Then came *Schindler's List*, and all bets were off. The movers and shakers were seized by genuine awe and admiration. Critics' organizations were similarly impressed, though still reluctant to give him full credit—one group awarded *Schindler's List* Best Film, but bypassed Spielberg for Best Director.

The conundrum was, to cite Elie Wiesel's often-quoted paradox: "How is one to tell a tale that cannot be—but must be—told?"

There are legitimate objections regarding the trickiness of images, which evoke instant and visceral responses, unlike words, which are so much more susceptible to authorial control. My own reservations, then and now, concern scenes of naked bodies, or, more precisely, naked extras, being herded into the gas chambers. These scenes have become so familiar as to be numbing, a kind of Holocaust pornography. For many, the first sight of such stomach-churning atrocities was Alain Resnais's terse, poetic, unforgettable *Night and Fog*, in 1955 one of the first films to document the horror. In these searing images, miraculously captured in the first place and somehow rescued from the devastation, it was real prisoners, not actors, who were marched to the crematoria, real skulls, hair, shoes, piled one upon another, real corpses plowed into the ground. If Resnais made his point through brevity, the opposite tactic was embraced thirty years later by Claude Lanzmann in *Shoah*, his epic retelling of the story through many voices and the background/foreground of Auschwitz-Birkenau and Treblinka. It is not to take anything away from these accomplishments to suggest that if there are deniers of the Holocaust, there are also its proprietors, artists like Lanzmann (quick to denounce Spielberg and other dramatists of the Final Solution) who so identify with the atrocity and its privileged singularity that they have come to believe it cannot be translated into another form—except theirs. Lanzmann is one; Art Spiegelman, who coined the term "Holokitsch," is another. For the masses of people who have not read *Maus* or seen Lanzmann's nine-and-a-half-hour film, for all of us, there is room for a more accessible telling of the story, and Spielberg has found it honorably. And, like so many politically charged movies based on true stories, license will be taken, and arguments will follow. Historians, pledged to the truth and nothing but the truth, will always disagree with critics, whose allegiance is to art, and the dramatic conventions that entails. Every film is a different case, and thoughtful viewers must decide for themselves if the freedoms taken are artistically valid.

Still, for me, the best scenes are oblique, suggestive, and all the more terrifying for that. The children being hauled away in those open trucks, shouting and waving and singing. Among the arrivals from Hungary being examined for their fitness to live, women prick their fingers, smear their lips and cheeks with their own blood in order to pass as healthy. German officers try to kill a poor one-armed worker in the courtyard of a factory, and the gun misfires and misfires and misfires, until finally the men walk away in disgust. Along the same lines is the mordantly funny scene of Goeth's hanging, when the chair refuses to topple, once, twice. We are reminded of the many screw-ups that, as much as luck and grit, allowed certain Jews to escape with their lives. This, to me, is where Spielberg's real brilliance lies: the light touches that underline the horror. More than the all-out emotional scenes, these are the way we acknowledge the enormity of what is happening just out of sight.

In the course of making *Schindler's List*, and in many interviews afterward, Spielberg acknowledged that he had now fully confronted his own Jewishness. He was about to turn fifty, and it was as if once he'd opened the doors, he could allow it all to come to the surface—stories and reminiscences about just how deeply the question of his Jewish identity had troubled his young life. Now all the stories his grandparents had told were finally connecting in a painful, visceral way, and the reality of it terrified him. He had known it would take ten years for him to make the film, and it did. It meant finding and acknowledging his place in the world.

But it was even more than that. If, in turning his life over to his rescue mission, Oskar was a man who found his calling, Spielberg also found through making this film something he was "meant to do."

The movie ends, somewhat controversially, in the present day and in color, with a parade of survivors representing those depicted in the film or their families, including the remarkable Pfefferberg. His presence is fitting, though one might still argue about Spielberg's decision to bring the story of *Schindler's List* out of its quasi-fictional framework into a real documented world. Into our world. But that transition away from art into the ethical realm represents a conscious decision on the part of the filmmaker as he embraces his new sense of mission.

The recording of the testimony of survivors would become the inspiration and the material of the Survivors of the Shoah Visual History Foundation. As Spielberg afterward described the genesis of the organization, a woman had come up to him during the shooting. The filmmakers had asked survivors to come to the set, to describe what they had witnessed. One woman seized his attention, speaking urgently, like the Ancient Mariner. Spielberg listened. She did not want to be in the film, as he at first assumed, but asked if he had a tape recorder. She wanted someone to listen to her memories and record them. She, and as it turned out countless others, had stories to tell, stories that would otherwise soon be buried with them.

It was this woman Spielberg credited with inspiring him to start the foundation, "the most important job I've ever done."[5] In 1994, he took what stretched into a three-year break from moviemaking to set up the foundation. An international team of interviewers, traveling into more than fifty countries, began collecting the stories of more than fifty-three thousand Holocaust survivors, in more than thirty languages, and compiling them into the Visual History Archive.

The foundation was seeded with six million dollars from the *Schindler's List* earnings, and budgeted at sixty million for the first three years. There were contributions from the Lew Wasserman Foundation, MCA Universal, Time Warner, and

NBC. Spielberg's contribution was part of the estimated forty million his Righteous Persons Foundation announced it would donate to various organizations in its first seven to ten years. It wasn't the only institution of its kind dedicated to remembrance: the U.S. Holocaust Memorial Museum, to which Spielberg's Righteous Persons Foundation donated six million, had opened eight months before the film. New York's Museum of Jewish Heritage and the Fortunoff Video Archive for Holocaust Testimonies at Yale were also parts of a vast rescue mission that would go some way to restoring the Jews to a history that had almost succeeded in expunging their names forever.

But the reach of Survivors of the Shoah lengthened, and its mandate expanded. As this massive undertaking came to fruition, the archive needed a more advanced form of digital preservation, and it moved in 2006 from Universal Studios to become part of the University of Southern California, renamed the USC Shoah Foundation—The Institute for Visual History and Education.

The foundation's website IWitness, launched in 2012, has become an extraordinary international educational resource, all the more valuable with each passing year, as survivors die. Teachers and students can register online, but through various branches and platforms, the foundation makes thousands of videographed testimonies available to all. Imaginatively interactive, testimonials may be followed by student dramatizations of the monologues just heard. There is something immensely moving—and heart-lifting—about watching teenagers solemnly (but also with a touch of play when called for) incorporate into their own lives the words of witnesses—soon to be history's ghosts.

Spielberg, though no longer the head of the foundation, still advises on all major decisions. In typically nonsectarian fashion he has widened the mandate of the Holocaust Foundation to include victims of other atrocities. In 2011 the foundation extended its scope to Rwandan victims, with plans to include Cambodia and Armenia.

This expanded agenda brought predictable complaints about the uniqueness of the Holocaust and the danger of "blurring" one group of victims with another. In this politically fraught arena, there is even controversy about the word "genocide," which some Jews believe should be used only to describe the Holocaust. The testimonies are crucial in so many ways, not just because the victims and even their children are dying off, but because so many were unable to talk at the time. There were vast silences and absences, and not just of the dead: Those who survived couldn't, or wouldn't, talk. They were free but they had nowhere to go. They feared hostility: they would be blamed for those who died, for surviving. They wanted to leave the camps behind them, forget and fit in, not burden their children . . . and suddenly—sometimes at great and painful cost—husbands and wives, widows and widowers, huddled in front of the camera, talked haltingly, wept.

From this point on, Spielberg saw his career differently. "I feel I have a responsibility. And I want to go back and forth from entertainment to socially conscious movies."[6]

During the three-year hiatus he didn't direct a movie but was busier than he'd ever been in his life. Along with two other industry hot shots, he started his own studio: DreamWorks, the dream child of Spielberg, Jeffrey Katzenberg (just departed from Disney), and the music impresario David Geffen. Formed in 1994, it was a rare and risky thing, a major studio built from the ground up. Like Charles Chaplin, Mary Pickford, Douglas Fairbanks, and D. W. Griffith when they started United Artists in the silent era, the DreamWorks founders saw themselves as artists opposed to the moneymen. It was Nicholas Beach all over again: they were going to change the rules, and if it had only been a matter of talent, media clout, bluster, and idealism, they would have.

Right from the start, practicality was lacking. With great fanfare, Spielberg, Katzenberg, and Geffen held a press conference to announce the start-up but disclosed no details, no specific film projects, just "a bucket of hype," in the words of DreamWorks chronicler Nicole LaPorte. Their mandate was to be "different" from other studios; they would make idiosyncratic films, even art house films, guided by taste rather than market dictates.[7]

DreamWorks' vicissitudes would be reported faithfully by the general press, which by now had made the fortunes and misfortunes of the movie business a major subject, a trend in which Spielberg had played a considerable part. It was perhaps the sense of the blockbuster mentality having gotten out of hand, ruling a movie industry to diminishing artistic returns, that inspired him to strike out and form a company with two egos as brash and successful as he was, but with a commitment to art.

Spielberg even broke his own vow never to invest in his own movies, and was having second thoughts almost as soon as the venture had gotten off the ground. He was actually a conservative investor, sinking most of his money in bonds, so that his net worth rose less rapidly but more solidly than most thrill riders of the stock market. He was worth three billion dollars, according to Forbes, ranking 205th in the world, and was one of the shrewdest businessmen in Hollywood when it came to his own contracts. Money wasn't the be-all and end-all, just the necessary validation of his worth in the high-stakes and very public casino of moviemaking. Yet with DreamWorks he had indeed gone off half-cocked, later acknowledging that the studio should have started gradually, one film at a time. He had violated his own pattern, what he called "the conservative, play-it-safe style that haunts me before I fall asleep at night."[8]

Envisioning the studio romantically as a kind of family-run campus for moviemaking, the trio had their eyes on a large tract of land that would include diverse kinds of housing along with cutting edge studio technology, an entertainment factory, a "media city of the future." But community resistance proved so intransigent that the plan had to be scuttled. Instead, the founders set up headquarters in Universal Studios, the old sandbox extending itself to accommodate them in fine enough fashion. There would be other limits on their grand, do-it-all blueprint. They would be forced to curtail plans to distribute their own films. There would be partnerships and distribution deals with other studios and entities, and an animation spin-off in 2004 under Jeffrey Katzenberg.

There would be Academy Award winners (*Saving Private Ryan*, *Shrek*, *Gladiator*, *American Beauty*—the last, one of the few "small" films). There would be blockbuster action films (*Transformers*) and a good number of flops. There would be rocky financial years, leading to a need for outside funding, and collaboration with other investors and attendant compromises.

And the movie business would prove bigger than any trio of individuals, however talented, the financing and distribution more unwieldy than in the day when studios controlled the theaters. What DreamWorks needed was that studio staple, experienced executives, administrators willing to do the daily work of running a business, planning and following through on a slate of productions. Spielberg was never engaged at that level. The projects on his multimedia agenda—video games and arcade centers—were failures as often as not, and the people he hired were oriented to prestige pictures, with little studio know-how. In addition, Kate had extracted a promise from him at the outset that he wouldn't turn into Katzenberg, an irredeemable workaholic; whether because he realized how such behavior had affected his first marriage, or because Kate brought it up during the conversation about her own future, he agreed.

It was just after Spielberg had told her of his plan to start DreamWorks. Kate had been trying out for some parts, hoping to renew her languishing career, and Spielberg wasn't happy at the prospect. At this point, the youngest of their children was two years old. The couple had been watching a rerun of *Indiana Jones and the Temple of Doom* on television when, according to her interview with Stephen Schiff, she turned to Steven and said, "'What happened to my career after that movie?' He said, 'You weren't supposed to have a career. You were supposed to be with me.'"[9] At which point she accepted the fact that she didn't have the all-out ambition to be an A-list actress. "My focus was on Steven and a large family." And the mutual pledge was made.

His fame by now was global. He already held the brass ring as the world's most successful movie entertainer *ever.* Now he'd earned respect on a global scale, winning awards (from Queen Elizabeth, among others), and traveling with *Schindler's List* to most of Europe.

He managed to keep his inner balance, but at a certain price. He became more and more withdrawn and secretive, even paranoid. After several horrifying threats to him and his family, he became extremely security conscious. He gave fewer interviews. He came home by six and on weekends he loved playing with the children. At the same time, his marriage to Kate also made him more open to intimacy, and for the first time in his life, he had a bunch of friends, "real buddies," Capshaw said. They were prominent in Hollywood, but not the wild or glamorous party guys. Instead, his close friends were one-time nerds like Robin Williams, Dustin Hoffman, Tom Hanks, and Robert Zemeckis, the ones who had been momma's boys and geeks of one kind or another, not popular in school, and who now bonded over family. As Hanks explained it, their outings didn't include sports, as either spectators or participants; they just hung out talking and "waiting to pick up our kids."[10]

But if Spielberg found new comfort in family and friends, the professional momentum, the cascade of ideas, the urge to keep making movies was undiminished. If anything, the break, and the difficulties with being a mogul, had brought him back with greater fervor to his calling as a director. It was time to make movies again, but his first would not be for DreamWorks. He'd secured an agreement with his partners whereby he could make movies for other studios, and he would start with *The Lost World: Jurassic Park* for Universal. He would, once again, go in two directions simultaneously. In line with his intention of making socially meaningful films, his first movie for DreamWorks would be the slave drama *Amistad.* The *Jurassic Park* sequel was an easy throw of the dice, *Amistad* a riskier bet—precisely one of those movies that he might sensibly have avoided, especially after the lashing of *The Color Purple.* But he figured that if he had acquired leverage, this was the time to use it. Spielberg had by now internalized the somewhat false bifurcation of the medium into art vs. money, the Serious vs. the Commercial, so that it became a self-fulfilling prophecy, a credo. On the one hand, he almost invited criticism by framing the "issue film" as good for you, something you had to take like castor oil, while belittling the popcorn movie as disposable, a summer throwaway. The irony is that if anyone had advanced the cause of taking "fun" genres seriously, it was Steven Spielberg.

13

Amistad and *The Lost World: Jurassic Park*

Never Say Never. Spielberg vowed he would never direct a sequel. He had refused to direct *Jaws II*, hated the idea of a spin-off of *E.T.* But he had already set a precedent with *Indiana Jones and the Temple of Doom.* Michael Crichton told fans who begged for a *Jurassic Park* follow-up that he wouldn't and couldn't. But the magnet of money and popular demand was irresistible, and, well, if they didn't make Son of *Jurassic Park*, someone else would. Crichton had cannibalized Arthur Conan Doyle's *Lost World* in writing his own trashy sequel, even borrowing his title.

But the dinosaurs, the raison d'être and pride of the first film, no longer staggered the imagination, and the characters were even less exciting. Richard Attenborough appeared again as the park impresario, along with a scientist-guest from the first film, Jeff Goldblum's mathematician and chaotician, plus a "behavioral paleontologist" partner, played by Julianne Moore.

There was more of everything: more violence, more noise, two Tyrannosaurus rexes instead of one, even more advanced CGI. But more wasn't better. Many considered *The Lost World* one of Spielberg's worst movies ever, but the franchise had its own momentum, and a sequel only had to go through the motions to hit the box office stratosphere. (This would be confirmed in 2015, when the neophyte Colin Trevorrow shepherded the artistically lackluster *Jurassic World* into the box office winner of the summer, with more than $639 million in domestic receipts.)[1]

In ironic counterpoint, Spielberg's first film for DreamWorks was anything but surefire. A critical and commercial failure (and, with *A.I.* and *Empire of the Sun* one of his most underrated efforts), *Amistad* dealt with the overthrow of a Portuguese slave ship in 1839 and its arrival in Connecticut, where the forty-four surviving Africans became stranded in jurisdictional limbo. It was a fascinating and even seminal piece of history: its myriad characters and courtroom perorations bring to the surface festering tensions over slavery, and executive and judiciary turf wars, that would soon convulse the country. As such the story of *Amistad* is a precursor not only to the Civil War but to the political and legal debate over slavery that would form the dramatic focus of Spielberg's *Lincoln*.

There were obstacles and opposition from the start, most prominently a lawsuit that turned the press against Spielberg before the film even began. Debbie Allen, a black producer and choreographer, who had come across the story while in college in 1978, pitched the idea to Spielberg in 1994. He was fascinated by the little-known tale, but he feared just the sort of backlash that had occurred with *The Color Purple*. In 1984, Allen optioned William A. Owens's 1953 novel *Black Mutiny: The Revolt on the Schooner Amistad*, continuing her campaign to get the story filmed. Then, in 1989, a novelized account, *Echo of Lions*, by Barbara Chase-Riboud, was coming out. Chase-Riboud submitted it to DreamWorks, which turned the project down. Later, when the novelist learned that the studio was making a film on the subject, she demanded ten million dollars for copyright infringement and screen credit.

There have been hundreds of such lawsuits—*Citizen Kane* was the subject of a similar litigation, eventually settled out of court. In the final script of *Amistad*, as in so many cases, one finds examples of passages that hew to an original idea, others that deviate widely from the supposed source, and still others that are simply part of recorded history and belong to us all. It is almost as hard to adjudicate such disputes as to sort out which writers did what in assigning screenwriting credits, with one or two standing in for the uncredited many.

Eventually DreamWorks was exonerated, but by the time Chase-Riboud withdrew her lawsuit (she eventually praised the film), much damage had been done to its credibility and that of its director. There were expressions of outrage by blacks and activists, coded versions of the familiar How Dare He?! Many were influenced, if not by the lawsuit, by the more general sense of Spielberg's presumption. One would have assumed that *Schindler's List* had earned him the right to deal with the oppression of minorities. Other reviewers tarred the film with the Stanley Kramer brush of earnestness and social uplift.

Seeing it again, I'm surprised at the harshness of the reviews. It's true that Spielberg, in this phase of his career, is given to didacticism, but the earnestness is always leavened by wit and his characteristic light touch. It may be that people weren't yet ready for a direct confrontation with slavery. A decade later race begins to be front and center: Lee Daniels's *The Butler* would win praise, and *12 Years a Slave*, a far more harrowing portrait of slavery than *Amistad*, would be embraced by audiences and win an Academy Award as Best Picture. Does time make that much difference? Or are audiences more inclined to sit still for guilt-inducing horrors when served up by a black filmmaker? In fact, Spielberg's film is far less punishing than Steve McQueen's, far more interested in nuance, in the way this terrible evil has metastasized into so many veins of our society.

The director surpasses his own reputation for spectacular openings in the drama of a slave ship at sea in a raging nighttime storm. As the boat heaves wildly, flashes of lightning expose a single black man emerging from the hold, gradually extracting a nail from the hull with which to unlock the chains of his comrades. Like the Omaha Beach scene in Spielberg's next picture, *Saving Private Ryan*, the whole violent, murky scene of overthrow is almost a miniature film in itself, a staggering piece of filmmaking in which the audience is caught up in the same confusion as the men. In a barrage of swords, fists, and shouts, of battling languages, the slaves attack the Spanish crew. The leader, Cinque, the "lion," is made to loom even larger, monumental and terrifying, as if all of Africa were rising up within this one figure, arms and voices finally freed to do battle, to vanquish the slavers and go home. Spielberg creates a rare bifocal vision so that we not only feel the long-buried anger erupting from the blacks but experience the Spaniards' point of view: the fruition of that nightmare of rebellion that kept white slave owners trembling in their beds at night and desperate to control their chattel by day.

As an outsider himself, Spielberg had always felt a kinship with blacks, an outrage at racial prejudice. He had an additional incentive: he and Kate had adopted two black children, bringing to seven their brood, and Spielberg particularly wanted to present this history lesson to his children, black and white.

There are echoes of the Holocaust in the sight of black slaves dying of hunger or thirst before they reach their destination. As in *Schindler's List*, we have the oppressed and their various would-be saviors, and as in *Lincoln*, we have the purists juxtaposed with pragmatists.

Amistad boasted an unusually wide array of male characters who provide an object lesson in early American history, a spectrum of the forces arrayed for and against the accommodation of slavery in the still-young democracy run by elites: the pious abolitionists, uncompromising in their refusal to negotiate; the pragmatic rascally attorney played by Matthew McConaughey, who (shades of Oskar) surprises everybody with his shrewd tactics; Morgan Freeman as the scholarly ex-slave and residing conscience; Anthony Hopkins playing possum as John Quincy Adams, a former president and the son of another, who (also like Oskar) is in Oedipal competition with a successful father.

An exceptionally strong supporting cast includes Pete Postlethwaite as a prosecuting attorney, Nigel Hawthorne as President Martin Van Buren, Arliss Howard as John C. Calhoun, and Austin Pendleton in a tiny but hilarious role as a linguist who can make nothing of the Mende language and finally simply fakes it and walks away. There are no caricatures; even John Calhoun is presented as cunning but reasonable-sounding, the voice of southern sovereignty, advancing in its most persuasive form the economic necessity argument.

Spielberg showed exceptional acuity in the casting of the Africans, who were uniformly well portrayed by actors in early career-making roles: Djimon Hounsou, as the formidable Cinque; Razaaq Adoti as Yamba; and as the liberated naval officer Ensign James Covey, Chiwetel Ejiofor, who, of course, would win an Academy Award for *12 Years a Slave*. Contrary to criticisms—the same sort that plagued *Schindler's List*—that the blacks were denigrated or depersonalized in comparison with the whites, the director gives the blacks as much prominence and individuality as he can without betraying history. And he shows the same silent film gift, on display in *Schindler's List*, for finding just the right face in a crowd, one that brings emotions to the surface. The person, often a woman, will make an impression in her one mute, memorable engagement with the camera.

Martin Amis defended the director's ability to pierce a grown man's heart with justifiable sentiment. I imagine his eyes welling at *E.T.*, while mine tear up at other scenes, notably one in *Amistad* that, illustrative of Spielberg's remarkable ecumenism, is a Christian one. The slaves have been given a Bible by the abolitionists, and after having studied it, Yamba introduces Christ's story to Cinque. Turning the pages and pointing to the pictures, he interprets Jesus's life and death: his holiness (signaled by the light around his head), his love of children, his death on the cross, and even his ascent into heaven. "Here is where his soul go when he die here," he tells Cinque, and, imagining the same fate for themselves, he concludes, "It's not so bad."

Some critics have complained that he infantilizes the blacks, but perhaps only Spielberg can understand the childlike quality of this universal yearning for grace, for a celestial home. There is real audacity, to my mind, in the way he honors, even identifies with, expressions of faith. Religious feeling seems to have no place in our ironic and secular age; even the word "icon" has lost its original, mystical power. Yet Spielberg goes where few directors dare, into the realm of faith and mystery.

The yearning for home that figures so prominently as a Spielberg theme derives its power from something akin to religious feeling. In *Amistad* that longing is only partially fulfilled on earth. The freed black Africans return to Sierra Leone, but as an afterword tells us, their land is riven by civil war, their families have been slaughtered. A terrible slave stronghold had been destroyed—along with many innocent people. And slavery lives on, on both sides of the Atlantic.

Yet Spielberg wants us to feel a sense of hope, that the past can affect the future. By paying homage to their ancestors, the great men who have preceded them, Cinque and Adams cast their lot with a future in which they have a stake, an optimistic belief that their accomplishment will be remembered, their sacrifice redeemed.

14

Saving Private Ryan and *A.I.*

If the opening of *Amistad* was intense, never had there been a battle scene as gut-wrenching as the D-day landing that opens *Saving Private Ryan*. Somewhere around this time was born the idea that movies had to be an "immersion" experience—undoubtedly with no small thanks to Spielberg himself. With *Jaws* we'd gotten our feet wet and our fears whetted. Now audiences were plunged without inflatable jackets into the amphibious landing on Omaha Beach, site of the most famous battle in World War II, a scene for which Spielberg used a thousand fake corpses and real amputees. All his filmmaking skills were on display, including but not restricted to the handheld camera. Cinematographer Janusz Kaminski uses a palette of desaturated color that is mostly gray, mud brown, and olive drab (the uniforms), then adds, as the battle progresses, vomit and viscera and splashes of red: blood splattered on the camera, the bloodshot eyes of soldiers, the sea turning crimson. Even the soundtrack goes silent, mimicking the temporary deafness of the soldiers under water and under fire. The action speaks not of victory but of confusion and loss.

Spielberg was prepared for the worst, figuring that if *Amistad* had alienated viewers, this would have them fleeing the theater in droves. Instead, the film became a hit, and not just a hit. Costing only $65 million (just $24 million more than *Amistad*), *Saving Private Ryan* racked up $479 million worldwide and won the Academy Award for Best Picture and Spielberg's second Oscar for directing.

It had to be a bit jarring, as it would be on subsequent occasions: first, the DreamWorks logo, the cerulean sky, little boy fishing from the crescent moon among puffy clouds, then boom, into a fog of war, where a platoon of terrified men fingering their crosses is plunging through mud and water toward shore.

The rest of the film followed a more conventional war-picture plot, pivoting on a commander's decision to dispatch a group of men into dangerous territory to save the only remaining member of a family of brothers. Spielberg got to make the war film that he'd dreamed of since Arnold began telling him stories of his service in Indonesia.

These vivid memories of connection were coming to displace those of negligence and disapproval. *Saving Private Ryan* was the movie that solidified the reconciliation between father and son. At his father's instigation, he and Tom Hanks would even produce a series about the war (Arnold's war) in Eastern Asia, *The Pacific*. It would run after their extremely successful HBO miniseries *Band of Brothers*.

Saving Private Ryan hadn't begun as a personal project—the script by Robert Rodat had come from an agent. But as always, Spielberg intuitively molded it to his own preoccupations, and by the time of the film's Oscar anointment, Spielberg was on stage sharing the honor with his father, to whom he had dedicated the film.

Tom Hanks as the schoolteacher-captain and Matt Damon as Ryan garnered superlative reviews. Critics who had been doubtful of Spielberg saw the film as "a watershed in emotional maturity," crediting Spielberg with finally trusting the audience and "manipulating them honestly."[1]

Some felt that after the spectacular twenty-four-minute Omaha Beach scene the rest of *Saving Private Ryan* was an anticlimax, a series of clichés. But a larger number were enthralled, right up until the film's sentimental ending. Janet Maslin in the *New York Times* found no letup in the film's "terrifying reportorial candor." "Imagine Hieronymus Bosch with a steadicam," she wrote. "Like the soldiers, viewers are made furiously alive to each new crisis and [are] never free to rest."[2]

Most problematic was the framing device: a man playing the elderly Ryan visits the cemetery where rows and rows of white crosses mark the graves of his comrades. The veteran's homage feels preachy, a superfluous attempt to underscore the film's patriotism. It was the "responsible" director abandoning art for a commemorative history lesson, telling us schoolchildren how to feel.

Saving Private Ryan also let Spielberg have it both ways ideologically, antiwar and appreciative of the "just" war, so that both sides could take a rooting interest. Yet the antihero and the outsider are profound parts of his emotional makeup. One of the most memorable scenes in *Private Ryan* concerns the soldier who hides, who ducks combat—the "coward" in the bunch, with whom Spielberg has said he identified. Indeed, even more gut-wrenching than the opening is the battle scene near the end in which the soldiers, now known to us, go at it in a merciless melee of deafening gunfire and terrifying silences, time stretched to infinity, as they grapple mano a mano, often killing one another in a confused, passionate embrace.

In paying tribute to his father's wartime experience, Spielberg's personal agenda once again coincided with the Zeitgeist.

Private Ryan was seen as an antidote to the Vietnam-induced gloom and cynicism in movies like *Apocalypse Now*. America was ready to celebrate the brave soldiers in a just war (a sentiment echoed simultaneously in Tom Brokaw's best-selling *The Greatest Generation*). Even those who had opposed the war were ashamed of how America had treated the returning soldiers after Vietnam, ignoring or ostracizing them.

The questionable ethics of the *Ryan* mission—sending six soldiers to their possible death in order to rescue one man—was raised but buried, as was the implication that the whole maneuver was a public relations move by the army. Such cynicism had no place in a Spielberg film. Even in much bleaker movies that came in the wake of global terror—*Minority Report*, *Munich*, *War of the Worlds*—there would be fear and pessimism, but never cynicism, and rarely the paranoia that was practically a default tone of the films of his contemporaries.

Nor was he interested in parceling out the nuances of history for their own sake. In 1998, he optioned A. Scott Berg's biography of Charles Lindbergh before it was published, and without having read it, presumably because he loved planes and had been drawn as a child to the pilot's feats of aviation. When he discovered the truth about the man—his dealings with the Nazis, his antisemitism, his double life—he began to dither. He commissioned several screenplays, vowing that he would do a warts-and-all movie, but it never came to pass. He had to connect emotionally with a subject, and the paradoxes of Schindler were about as far as he could go.

Stephen Jay Gould was not the only one who had been bowled over by the sophistication of the dinosaurs in *Jurassic Park*. In his hideaway in England, Stanley Kubrick was contemplating a futuristic film about a robot, a child who has been programmed to love his adoptive parents, but who yearns to become human so that his mother will return his love. The idea came from a 1969 short story by Brian Aldiss, which Kubrick optioned in 1982. "Super-Toys Last All Summer Long" takes place in a future in which the earth has been decimated by floods, with the remnants of civilization fighting for survival. Pregnancies are restricted by lottery, resources are scant, and a number of tasks are performed by robots, called mechas, who, in the film's bleakly apocalyptic ending, will survive man and salvage the planet.

So far, standard sci-fi, if rather more finely imagined than most. But the real heart of the film, absent from the original story, is the tale of the robot child and his mother, and the former's Pinocchio-like quest to become human.

The idea of using Carlo Collodi's famous 1883 fairy tale as a model originated with Kubrick—and led to a break with Brian Aldiss over the screenplay. After Aldiss exited, Kubrick had developed a book-length treatment with science-fiction writer Ian Watson that featured fifteen hundred stunning illustrations by the conceptual artist Chris Baker. This would become, in effect, the shooting script, the graphics a crucial link between Kubrick's early conception and Spielberg's later one. (Other writers who collaborated with Kubrick were Bob Shaw, Arthur C. Clarke, and Sara Maitland.)

But the director was at an impasse. He wanted a robot to play David, but the technology did not yet exist. He discussed the problem with Spielberg, with whom he'd become friends and telephone pals over the years. They would talk for hours, on Kubrick's time and terms (he called collect), the older man quizzing Spielberg on everything imaginable, and giving nothing in return. Spielberg called this latest father figure a "benevolent inquisitor."[3]

Spielberg had been surprised when Kubrick first brought up the Aldiss story, and told the younger man he was interested in making a film. They discussed it at great length. At one point, Kubrick, who increasingly thought Spielberg would be the right director, even suggested some sort of collaboration, but Spielberg was too much of a control freak to work with anyone else. (It was bad enough, he would say later, to have been haunted by Kubrick's "ghost" on the set.) Were the CGI techniques used for *Jurassic Park* advanced enough to produce a robot boy? Kubrick even consulted with the supreme dinosaur architect, Dennis Muren, and some of the technicians at Industrial Light and Magic who had worked on *Jurassic Park.*

From these discussions, Kubrick realized that the technology couldn't yet accomplish what he wanted, while it became equally clear that he couldn't use a human: the robot had to remain the same from beginning to end, and a human child would simply grow too much in the time it took the notoriously exacting director to make the film. After he died in 1999, leaving boxes full of papers with the drawings and ideas, Spielberg, urged by Kubrick's executors, seized the reins. He took the project to Warner, wrote a screenplay himself from Watson's screen story, and ended up assuming full screenwriting credit.

The Pinocchio model, if it had alienated Kubrick from the creator of the story that was *A.I.*'s source, was just one instance of the complex melding of his sensibilities with those of the director to whom he would entrust his vision. The great Disney film version of *Pinocchio* was deep in Spielberg's DNA. "When You Wish upon a Star" had hovered over *Close Encounters,* considered for a time as its theme; it threaded through other John Williams scores for Spielberg films as well.

When *A.I. Artificial Intelligence* was released, critics failed to understand this vital connection and accused Spielberg of betraying Kubrick's vision. Having categorized the two directors as polar opposites, they assumed that Spielberg was responsible for the "sentimental" parts, Kubrick for the movie's harsher aspects. Where the sentimentality is to be found in this story of a child being abandoned by its mother is hard to fathom. The film does have its tonal discrepancies, but, as with *Empire of the Sun*, cuteness has disappeared from Spielberg's palette. In *A.I.*, horror, anguish, and very dark humor are the dominant colors, and from all accounts Spielberg embraced Kubrick's conception and script, while adding a certain warmth—just as Kubrick had hoped.

A couple whose son lies in a coma acquire a robot child, a mecha, brought by Henry (Sam Robards) from the factory to comfort his wife, Monica (Frances O'Connor), in her loneliness. David, played with uncanny solemnity by Haley Joel Osment, is supernaturally obedient and devoted to his mother, but longs for her love in return. O'Connor, trying and failing to warm to him, gradually, guiltily recoils from his eerie presence. When their biological son Martin returns, chaotic undercurrents threaten to capsize the family. An Oedipal struggle between father and foster child ends with Henry insisting that they get rid of David. In a wrenching scene of abandonment, Monica drives David out into the country and leaves him to fend for himself, simply hoping that he will join up with other mechas like himself. As guide and companion, David has only his Teddy, a supertoy both cuddly and wise.

Once branded by the couple, David can't be returned to the factory. And having failed to win a place in the family, he determines to search, like the wooden Pinocchio, for the Blue Fairy who will transform him into a human being, so that he can finally earn his mother's love.

A searing fable of rejection, yet why should critics have been so surprised? Not only were there fractured and broken families, not only were there victims of prejudice and persecution, but now the maturing director had widened his vision to include mankind's tendency to cruelty throughout history, an evil consummated in the Holocaust and in his own *Schindler's List.* Moreover, this was a particular interest of the Jewish Kubrick, who had at one time considered making a film about the Holocaust. Enter the Flesh Fair, a lurid netherworld, a free-for-all of prostitution and willful incarceration into which the abandoned David stumbles. Here, in a conscious echo of the Final Solution, humans demonize and systematically exterminate the mechas. Kubrick was particularly concerned with this section, figuring the sequence had already earned the movie an automatic R rating, and trusting Spielberg to find a way to make it palatable to an audience.

Many found the section a misstep, and certainly this strange interlude, a scary *Walpurgisnacht* given a certain jaunty panache by Jude Law's Gigolo Joe, occupies a different order of sensory horror, and has a hard time competing with the drama of a child's yearning for mother love. Still, in a film that envisions the wreckage that man has made of his planet, the Flesh Fair seems like a fairly accurate parable of what humanity is serving up daily in the form of murderous cults, Kalashnikov-wielding teenagers, a culture of exploitation, greed, and corruption at every level. At least as seen through the prism of Kubrick's decidedly un-rose-colored glasses.

Spielberg probably did, as one critic suggested, "soften Kubrick's misanthropy" (he introduced the Gigolo Joe character), but not by much. In interviews, he bristled at what he took to be reductive and wrongheaded views of himself and Kubrick, maintaining to critic Joe Leydon that "all the parts of *A.I.* that people assume were Stanley's were mine. And all the parts of *A.I.* that people accuse me of sweetening and softening and sentimentalizing were all Stanley's. The teddy bear was Stanley's. The whole last 20 minutes was completely Stanley's. . . . It was Stanley who did the sweetest parts of A.I. not me. . . . I'm the guy who did the dark center of the movie, with the Flesh Fair and everything else. That's why he wanted me to make the movie in the first place. He said 'this is much closer to your sensibilities than my own.'"[4]

An exaggeration, perhaps, but what most couldn't appreciate was the degree to which the film was both deeply personal and deeply Kubrickian at the same time. Sara Maitland, a British writer who combined religion, feminism, and magic realism in her short stories, had been brought in to enhance the fairy-tale aspects of the story. In addition, she and Kubrick had had long conversations about motherhood. Each director was drawn to the tragic theme of parental neglect, and they shared a fascination with other forms of life. In addition, both were drawn to the supernatural, to mystery and fable, an approach both felt was more in tune with the times than naturalism. And Spielberg by now had arrived at a place where he could see the points of view of both parent and child, all of which contribute to the distressingly powerful tensions between David and Monica.

In attacking the assumptions of the press, Spielberg wanted, once and for all, to dispense with the charge of sentimentality. Indeed, the film derives its haunting nature from an abiding dread, a profound sense of uncertainty—Monica's and ours—as to the nature of this humanoid. How deep does his programming go, and what is this love he offers? Is David's expressed attachment just the mechanical cheeriness of the most advanced version of Siri?

If David can love, does that mean he has a soul, free will? Or are both of these concepts obsolete? And how can there be love without intelligence, without self-questioning, without hate?

Separation anxiety, a mother's death: the film seems to sum up all the potential failures and terrors in a mother-child relationship from a child's point of view, but it also touches on the darkly subversive apprehension a woman can harbor toward motherhood—wanting and not wanting a child, the dread of childbirth itself, or fear of a "defective" or even a "different" child, an unlovable child. And isn't there something almost too unwavering, too insistent, too nonnegotiable, about David's love and compliance?

In an almost parodic sense David is a dream child: a poster child for ecology, he consumes not nor does he make waste. He needs no babysitter, he doesn't get sick or sleep (so he can't have bad dreams), he obeys all commands, and he can't be traumatized—except, apparently, by desertion. It's almost a relief when David does something terrifying (in Monica and Henry's eyes), cutting off her hair for a keepsake with scissors deliberately made to gleam with Hitchcockian menace.

Studies have shown that the more closely a robot resembles a human, the more we are repelled. David unnerves us because we can't place him definitively on one or the other side of the human/machine divide. Kubrick surely intended this chilling ambiguity, while also sensing that Spielberg would turn David into someone an audience would—if not love, at least care about, feel attached to almost unwillingly. He teeters like a parody between the real and unreal. When he laughs, the sound is grotesque, its sci-fi artificiality all too suggestive of the mystery and creepiness of kid humor. When he opens the bathroom door to see his mother sitting on the toilet—something every child does, though not usually to a horror-filled shriek—there is no special curiosity; he sees her sitting on what might as easily be a chair. Or so we assume, as he has no lower body activities of his own to learn to repress, hide, despise, or feel shame for. No penis to make him wonder whether his mother is similarly equipped.

His robotoxed face never changes, but the boy erupts with "love," seethes with what feels like sibling rivalry. When the "real" son Martin comes home, David begins shoving spinach in his mouth. But having no bodily functions, he breaks down—or clogs up—and has to have surgery. It's like the scene when

E.T. gets drunk, except that that one is charming, while this one is ghastly.

Near the end of the film, another scene of violence: suddenly there appears a chorus line of robots exactly like David, but newer, and in a paroxysm of rage, he tries to smash them to smithereens. One of the most lyrical and disturbing images of *A.I.* occurs in a swimming pool at a children's birthday party, when a roughhousing David nearly drowns Martin. The latter has been rescued and is being fussed over by everyone, while David drifts, unnoticed and unattended, toward the bottom of the pool. We are left in ignorance as to the meaning and source of David's actions. If he is afraid, what constitutes a "fatal" danger? Is it water damage to his hard drive, or maternal rejection? In its eerie ontological fluidity, David's submersion looks forward to the arresting image in *Minority Report* of the "precogs," prophets of the future, floating in their amniotic pool. Questions hover, unanswerable, about the foreignness of children, and what it means to be human.

In the books Kubrick devoured as he was thinking about *A.I.*, scientists were forecasting a genetic takeover by robots, predicting that our immortality would lie (as is indicated in the film) in the "transplanting of our minds into superior machine intelligences." In this haunting film, a case is being made for the gentle takeover of mankind by its own inventions. These are not fire-breathing Godzillas, trampling buildings and cars and bringing Armageddon, but benign Frankensteins saving us (or some shred of us) from ourselves. We are invited to witness our demise almost as a consummation devoutly to be wished. Like Hal in *2001: A Space Odyssey*, the robots are more sympathetic than the humans. The new "line" of robots are figures of grace, emerging from their chrysalis of Giacometti-like sylphs, presumably less prone to the ego trips and irrationalities of humans like Monica and David, or the scientist played by

William Hurt. Our tools are extensions of ourselves, our faces masks at the best of times, and as the film sees it, a depersonalization is already taking place. How "real" is Monica, after all? David, by freezing Monica's emotions, brings her into the android sphere.

It wasn't hard for Kubrick to relish the end of the human race: he'd never been that attached to it in the first place. More concerned with our responsibility toward our robots than with theirs toward us, he urges us to "be kind to them." In an interview he gave the *New York Times* in 1968 he said, "There's no doubt that there's a deep emotional relationship between man and his machines, which are his children. But then one day they will walk away from us old parents and seek their own future."[5]

Neither Kubrick nor Spielberg was drawn to the interplay of flesh-and-blood adults, the complexities of human psychology; not for them the entanglements of eros. Even other robots are sexier than theirs. In his one "erotic" film, *Eyes Wide Shut*, Kubrick captures the coldness of eros but not its heat. An indifference to human pleasures, and their seat in irrationality, makes him predisposed to prefer machines.

We humans are a lost cause; our only hope is as a figment of memory—David's. The movie's ending is poignantly and explicitly Proustian. Kubrick had been reading *In Search of Lost Time* as he was contemplating the film, and he felt an immediate sympathy with the French writer's idea of memory as an artificial construct, occupying another dimension of time. David's search will ultimately lead him—worlds and life cycles later—to the beginning of *Swann's Way:* a mother and son and a bedtime kiss.

As their two heads lie on the pillow, David is consciously fashioning an image, one he will take through all eternity, of "perfect" mother love, uninterrupted by competition from the father, from siblings, from reality. This ecstatic fantasy of perfect oneness is of course a kind of death: a one-sided dream that exists only in David's imagination. For the mother is long gone, and their union belongs to the virtual world of memory and dream.

Spielberg didn't have to read Proust to be on the same wavelength. He understood the subjective delusions of love, and that the perfect family exists only in a child's wishful imagination. In a striking early scene—a version of Spielberg's on-the-outside-looking-in signature shot—the newly arrived David wanders through his adoptive home, examining everything in sight. His eye falls upon a family portrait of Monica, Henry, and Martin—and mirrored by the glass, he inserts himself into the picture, making the trio a foursome. The shot will have an uncanny echo two years later, in Spielberg's *Catch Me If You Can*, when Leonardo DiCaprio's pilot-imposter returns "home" to his mother on Christmas Eve and looks through a picture window, only to discover that his place in the bosom of the family has been usurped by a half-sister. And he's looking back at himself.

15

Minority Report and *Catch Me If You Can*

Not only had Spielberg received honors in all parts of the globe, but his philanthropic contributions were equally international in scope. He was giving millions, much of it anonymously, to a variety of causes, most notably Jewish and health-related organizations. He had started his philanthropic activities as a kid, when he donated proceeds from his home screenings to a local charity, and now his interests ran from the Survivors of the Shoah Visual History Foundation, and his Righteous Persons Foundation (which donates money to Jewish organizations and historical projects that relate to the Holocaust), to disaster relief (Darfur), education (USC), and medical research. In 1997, after a large bequest, a wing for pediatric medicine at Cedars-Sinai Medical Center was named after him.

Donations were made jointly by Spielberg and Capshaw, both names on the plaque. Kate, a talented painter, was studying at the Art Students League; the marriage was to all appearances a great success. The couple had become a power team on the political front as well, backing the opposition to Proposition 8 (which had banned gay marriage in California), and Steven even resigned from his beloved Boy Scouts over the issue of discrimination against gays. The Spielbergs had been contributing to local and national Democratic candidates for some years, and during the 2008 election, he gave money to both Hillary Clinton and Barack Obama, wavering between the two and finally, to the distress of the Clintons, settling on Obama. The fund-raising events and financial backing by Spielberg and his DreamWorks partners was thought to be crucial in persuading California liberals to switch from Clinton to Obama.

Yet despite this apparent visibility, he was withdrawing ever more from public life. A horrifying episode with a stalker had come to a head when the man—a would-be screenwriter with a van full of Spielberg tapes and logos, a rape kit, and the names of his seven children—was arrested (for the second time!), tried, and convicted for felony stalking, with a sentence of twenty-five years to life. Although there would continue to be intrusions, this lurker's threats were the most upsetting: he claimed to be Spielberg's adopted son and planned to rape him in front of his wife.

Spielberg had gone, as his friend the screenwriter Bob Gale pointed out, from the innocent and trusting child in *E.T.* to a version of the isolated boy, restless and wary, in the prison camp in *Empire of the Sun.* As if such personal anxieties were not enough, on September 11, 2001, suicide terrorists crashed four airplanes, two into the World Trade Towers. A sense of paranoia and apprehension gripped the nation, and 9/11 would play a large part, either explicitly or on a subterranean level, in Spielberg's subsequent movies. His next film, *Minority Report,* based loosely on an early Philip K. Dick fable, was made to order for a man privately obsessed with security but equally worried, like many of us, about the overreach of its enforcers.

He had been looking into the story's possibilities long before the World Trade Center attacks and the expansion of government surveillance that ensued. But in the way he adapted the tale to present circumstances, the director again showed his instinctual sense of the national mood. George W. Bush took office in 2001 and instituted the controversial U.S. Patriot Act, under the direction of Attorney General John Ashcroft. The National Security Agency and the Federal Bureau of Investigation would now be allowed to collect data indiscriminately from phone companies and other corporations, not just on "persons of interest" but on an entire citizenry, in case someone might pose a problem in the future. In *Minority Report*, "precogs" supply a special police unit with data on crimes, past, present, and future, a conceit that addresses questions not only of determinism and free will, but of preventive detention as well.

Spielberg was in tune with the Zeitgeist to an unnerving and even unmanning degree: when the film came out and seemed to coincide almost too closely with the government's post-9/11 policies, the director, not wanting to appear unpatriotic at such a critical time, distanced himself from the film's implicit controversy, endorsing the Bush administration's measures.

But the real attraction of the film was precisely the sleekly terrifying dystopia it so coolly and gorgeously visualized, a semihuman world of a future (2054) that seemed all too contemporary. The nonacademic schoolboy who had resisted his father's field of science and technology and had instead pursued the path of fantasy and storytelling was by now something of a techno wizard himself. An early video gamester and pioneer in cutting-edge CGI, he had become more than complicit in that machine-made future both imagined and dreaded by science fiction movies, a prime mover in the transition to a machine-made environment, by which human nature (as well as cinema) was redefining itself.

Were the movies' first hundred years but an episode in the development of animation? asks critic J. Hoberman, seeing the director at the center of a revolutionary—or evolutionary—change in our sense of the cinematic "real."[1] Scholar James Naremore expressed a similar reaction to the computerized world of *A.I.*[2] Immensely moved by the story, he was nevertheless troubled: he marveled that a movie that so effectively asks what it means to be human is itself such a mountain of artifice, with its endless end credits listing a battalion of technical specialists and digital experts from Industrial Light and Magic and Public Data Images.

After an extraordinary beginning that is like a high-tech update of *Rear Window*, the movie settles into an extended chase as John Anderton (Tom Cruise), chief of the Precrime Unit, tries to find the perpetrator of his son's kidnapping and presumed murder some years earlier—a disappearance that also ripped apart his marriage. He anxiously pores over old home videos—his son racing to him, his wife in nightdress begging him to stop recording her. Watching, editing, pulling significant images, he becomes, as critics noted, the director of a movie within the movie, pulling out all the stops, showing his tech bag of tricks.

A soaringly spiritual score—Tchaikovsky, Schubert, and Haydn, and, on the organ, Jesu, Joy of Man's Desiring—speaks to the sublimity of Spielberg, and mankind's, aspirations, but the aspirations are mocked by the soulless pursuit of safety and convenience on which humankind is embarked.

No sooner has Anderton embarked on his quest than he himself is targeted by those very precogs as a murder suspect, himself now the object of a manhunt. The spectacle of flight itself takes on personal overtones, as if Spielberg himself, the road runner, were trying to outrun his own inventions, to find/restore his "home," not just at work, but with his wife and son. "Gotta keep running," says Anderton's boy in the video, and the father replies, "Gotta keep running."

Critic Geoffrey O'Brien suggests that Anderton's expulsion from the Precrime Unit resembles nothing so much as the terror a filmmaker might feel at losing his job, being evicted from his studio.[3] As it happens, or as *would* happen, a year later—in an occurrence only a precog might have foreseen—Spielberg was to experience precisely that kind of expulsion from paradise, when a financially troubled DreamWorks appealed to and was rejected by Universal, Spielberg's "home" studio. He sank into a rare depression.

Spielberg has said his films always have to *arrive* someplace, often that place of arrival is a rendition of home. In a flimsily hopeful ending, *Minority Report* reaffirms free choice, and the family bond is restored, but the pro forma conclusion lacks conviction and is at odds with the propulsive energy of the sci-fi fantasy that has preceded it.

The family scene in a lakeside cabin, far from radiating "so much love," generates no warmth at all, possibly because the family is now a childless couple, hence—in Spielberg's core belief—no family at all. The assertion of love comes from Agatha (Samantha Morton), a precog now restored to the world of humans, visiting Anderton and his wife. But humanity takes a further hit in the loss we feel at her transformation from incandescent seer to ordinary woman, peddling a hollow vision of love.

The home that Spielberg's films about childhood cherished, in all their fractiousness, has become ever more elusive. Yet the yearning is no less powerful for that, as deeply embedded in the director's psyche as that of a homing pigeon. The home, no longer a real place, becomes a memory—part

Forger and father figure: Leonardo DiCaprio and Tom Hanks in *Catch Me If You Can.* DreamWorks Distribution/Photofest

real, part fantasy—of a family before divorce, the holy trinity of mother, father, and child together at Christmastime in *Catch Me If You Can*, a movie Spielberg himself has acknowledged as his most personal. A comedy of mixed moods, mostly dismissed by critics as frivolous, a "palate cleanser" between important movies, the story is that of the real life forger and impersonator, Frank Abagnale Jr.

Starring Leonardo DiCaprio as Frank, Christopher Walken and Nathalie Baye as his parents, *Catch Me If You Can* feels as if it was made on the fly, and it was—in an unheard-of fifty-two days, and with more than twice that many locations. DiCaprio had a cold and was miserable during the shooting, which may have contributed to the feeling of physical and mental exhaustion toward the end, as the struggle to maintain a façade becomes intolerable, and the impostor runs out of gas.

The "perfect" marriage of his odd-couple parents—the fast-talking chiseler dad and the graceful French wife he managed to snare after the war—begins to dissolve after the father's indictment on tax fraud has forced them to move to an apartment in Queens. Just as the Spielbergs' divorce catapulted Steven from the family nest, so young Frank, forced to choose, becomes an orphan on the run.

For all its lightness of spirit—and the film races and soars and eludes pursuit as if lit up by a James Bond martini—there is a deep substratum of melancholy. Christmas hovers over the whole film as the saddest night of the year for the two loners: Frank and his nemesis, Carl Hanratty, the plodding FBI agent played by Tom Hanks, divorced, his ex-wife and daughter living in another city.

The deft screenplay, by Jeff Nathanson, is based on Abagnale's memoir, but incorporates important changes. The real Frank Jr., for example, never saw his father again, but here the father continues to play a role in the life of his son, who can't let go of the hope of a reunion between his parents.

Another change: in the movie, the mother has a lover—also absent from the original. The "good family friend," like Leah's Bernie Adler, comes over when Dad's at work, and eventually marries the adulterous wife. The son is not only expelled from paradise but perhaps sexually traumatized as well: the very day he discovers his mother's betrayal, Frank has raced home full of excitement, about to tell her he's fallen for a girl at school. Then he sees the lover in the bedroom and goes quiet. That's the last we hear of that girl, and it will take him a while to lose his virginity, eventually to a stewardess—someone as much on the fly as he is.

There were other personal themes as well: *Catch Me* is a fable about acting and masquerade, about "passing," something a Jewish guy growing up in the heartland and trying to hide his ethnicity would know something about. Another is that of the imposter, the classic fear shared by many high achievers, that it is all a fraud. Spielberg's success had to feel outrageous, disproportionate. "I'll be caught out," the fearful sufferer thinks, as he flees some version of the "law," all those people who "know" the truth, who can see through his ruse.

Some critics were bothered by the movie's blithe-seeming endorsement of a felon—a criminal, moreover, whose punishment is in fact a reprieve: he becomes an assistant to the FBI in tracking down forgers like himself, then graduates to entrepreneurship. That dissonance was reinforced by the casting of the baby-faced DiCaprio. Scorsese would tap into that same ambiguity by starring him as the "charming" criminal in *The Wolf of Wall Street.* What the actor brings to both films is a lovely, baffled, lost-child quality. And for Spielberg, the emotional isolation Frank experiences would be a far greater retribution than imprisonment.

The New York conjured up by the magical production design (Jeannine Oppewall) and the witty costumes of Mary Zophres is a decade and a city high on its own possibilities—a city (my city) of the *Mad Men* era that seemed like a fantasy even at the time, in which budding "career girls" had just moved to New York, had landed jobs, and were in seventh heaven. On a beginning salary you could afford an apartment (with a roommate), you would be taken to eat occasionally at one of the great restaurants and often at the mere bistros, you would proudly deposit your weekly salary in one of the grand, vaulted nineteenth-century banks, all wood and brass with friendly tellers, and you would walk in style down Madison Avenue as if you owned the world. You could participate in the New York of elegance, could dress well without undue expense, could put on a front. The sixties coiffures, bouffant or Vidal Sassoon, the phalanx of the Pan Am personnel, stewardess babes and virile pilots marching through the airy Saarinen-style terminals like Rockettes and rock stars—the skies are friendly indeed to a handsome teenager who looks like a Greek god in uniform. Barriers could be breached, bridges crossed, and refugees from elsewhere in America, including even the outer boroughs, could make it in the Big Apple if they were smart enough, bold enough, and wore the right clothes.

Or so it seemed.

Frank learns early the importance of putting up a front. After his father's financial ruin and relocation of the family from Long Island, Frank Jr. becomes the object of ridicule because he's wearing a prep school blazer at a scruffy inner-city high school.

His first successful impersonation, when he jumps to fill in for a French teacher in a high school class, lands him in hot water but propels him on a career path unimagined by the average vocational counselor. As a fairly innocent identity thief, he poses in succession as an airline copilot, a lawyer, even an emergency room doctor (*Marcus Welby, M.D.* was his instruction manual).

He falls for a deceptively dewy Lutheran nurse played by the enchanting and as yet unknown Amy Adams—yet another example of Spielberg's eye for talent ready to break out. Passing himself off as a lawyer to her district attorney father (Martin Sheen), he marries and finds the surrogate family he's been looking for in her Bible-quoting and mutually adoring father and mother. The usually alert Frank stops running, blinded by bliss. He is caught, and flees once again, this time to Montrichard, France, the home of his mother.

It is Christmas Eve, Frank has once more landed—briefly and somewhat dubiously—on his feet, making money (literally) in a printing plant in Montrichard. But Hanratty is on his tail. He's arrested by the French police, and shortly thereafter he's on a plane, safely in the agent's custody (or so it would seem), when Hanratty informs him of his father's death. Devastated, he slips into the restroom and performs another Houdini-like disappearing trick, dropping through the hold as the plane is landing. From here, he makes his way to the Long Island home of his mother, and the Christmas Eve "nativity" scene that is being held with his replacement, a half-sister. It's all over. He turns and surrenders. The Road Runner has reached the abyss.

Like the real Abagnale, he will be imprisoned, but then employed as a forger-detector by the FBI. The real Frank Abagnale married, had children, and made millions, we're told, as a self-employed forgery detective. The fictional Frank will be stuck in an office, or on the road in an old model car with Carl, pursuing low-level crooks, sharing a beer on weekends and at Christmastime.

It goes without saying that Frank will occasionally try to run and Carl will always bring him back. From here on in, they are chained together like two halves of the same man, which indeed they are: the hopelessly yearning child in Spielberg and the earnestly mature man of integrity. And from here on in, a lot of what you think about Spielberg will be keyed to what you feel about Tom Hanks, his friend and, increasingly, his alter ego.

16

The Terminal, War of the Worlds, *and* Munich

In *The Terminal*, another comedy threaded with darkness, featuring another man who wants to go home, Tom Hanks plays Viktor Navorski, a traveler from eastern Europe who upon his arrival at JFK learns that his country, Krakozhia, has undergone a revolution and officially no longer exists. The no-man's land into which Viktor now falls mirrors Spielberg's own feeling of being adrift.

As Spielberg was making the film, Hollywood was in an increasingly conservative mood, reinforced by wildly escalating costs—this at the very time that DreamWorks was trying to get off the ground. It had taken three years for the studio to release its first movie, *The Peacemaker*, a formulaic thriller about nukes poised to attack New York City. There had been a string of prestige hits, with Academy Awards three years in a row for, respectively, *American Beauty*, *Gladiator*, and *A Beautiful Mind*. But the last two were coproductions with Universal, and the brand was further diluted by increasing dependence on outsiders for funding or distribution. Diversification could absorb some risks, but the studio's slate of movies was all over the place, following no particular principle, artistic or otherwise: an uncategorizable mix of horror films, disaster films, and schlock comedy—"junk food cinema," with the occasional true original, most often from Jeffrey Katzenberg's animation department. *Antz* was followed in 2001 by *Shrek*, the jewel in the crown.

Spielberg was now a mogul, and perhaps not very good at it, being first and foremost a filmmaker. But crucial to him was that he was working for himself and his own studio rather than for others, as he had all of his life. When he was making *Amistad* and *A.I.*, which he thought of almost as "experimental films," he described himself to a reporter for the *Times* of London as "an independent working in the Hollywood mainstream."[1]

At the same time, a lot was going on in his life: besides his disappointment with the failure of DreamWorks to take off and frustration with the movie business in general, he was beset by losses and personal anxieties, not least over the security threats to his family. As there were always naysayers ready to pounce, he must have felt isolated and friendless, and *The Terminal* would both reflect and reinforce his sense of vulnerability.

Spielberg has created a visual tour de force—a busy, Breughel-like tapestry, a modern fable of humanity in the fallen state of twenty-first-century air travel. The movie may have failed to astound viewers precisely because its setting is both so familiar and so fraught.

Tom Hanks gives one of his most charming performances as the tourist who speaks no English (he learns of the coup from images on the airport's ubiquitous TV monitors). Unable to communicate or understand what has happened to him, he becomes an embarrassment to the customs officials who peer down on the floor from a glass enclosed aerie, like scientists observing lab rats.

The Armageddon theme that runs through Spielberg's later films—the sense of America as bully, warmonger, and despoiler of the planet—has its least oblique rendering in *War of the Worlds*, a rare Spielbergian swerve into dystopia and a study in chaos, with America on the receiving end of an alien invasion. The classic fable by H. G. Wells, in which Martians land in rural England, had been made into a film in 1953 (also set in America, and drawing on Cold War fears), but Spielberg uses his extreme moviemaking skills to turn it into a terrifying nonstop action-horror film. This time, in a reversion to the tone of the fifties sci-fi films he grew up on, and perhaps allowing the dark underside of his kid-friendly early films to emerge undiluted, the extraterrestrials are anything but friendly. The natives are none too sympathetic either: as they run for their lives, they turn on one another and descend into brutish inhumanity. At one point the "hero," the father played by Tom Cruise, has to kill a man who is threatening his daughter. At the center is the proverbial family story: even as the planet is threatened with extinction, this lapsed father, heretofore a model of irresponsibility, finds redemption in trying to save his children. This time critics found the equation out of kilter: the disproportionate focus on family when the whole world is going to wrack and ruin came to seem, as A. O. Scott said, like "very expensive family therapy."[2]

Tom Cruise once again puts a lot of mileage on his running shoes, but the movie is heavy going, with none of the wit and comic relief we've come to expect even in Spielberg's darker films. Nevertheless, Cruise and Spielberg made a bundle on the film, which became a box office hit, grossing $591.7 million worldwide.[3]

Spielberg was known as a shrewd negotiator, even a harsh

one. His sister Anne, as close as they were, confessed that she was leery of negotiating with him. He had set a precedent with the first Indiana Jones film, when he dug in his heels to establish the terms according to which he was still getting paid, not up front, as was customary, but out of the gross—a percentage that had jumped from twenty to a whopping fifty, way more than even the biggest star. As a consequence, he and Cruise made a total of seventy million dollars from *Minority Report*, as against a paltry twenty million each for Twentieth Century-Fox and DreamWorks.

Long before 9/11, the massacre of eleven Israeli athletes and coaches at the 1972 Munich Olympics may have been the opening volley in the "holy war" of modern terrorism. Spielberg and his father watched on television, horrified as masked gunmen broke into the dormitory and took the athletes hostage, then killed them in a fusillade at the airport. The director said it was the first time he heard the word "terrorist."

The shock was profound at the sight of Jews once again being killed in Germany. Still, Spielberg probably wouldn't have touched a subject so fraught with politics and passion except that after 9/11 his worldview had shifted, along with his mood. A powerful sense of his country in peril, both from outsiders and from itself, now dictated his mission as a filmmaker. With so many blockbusters behind him, he was privileged to pick and choose subjects that were more serious, less obviously commercial.

An odd assortment of individuals with varying skills and levels of commitment, handpicked by Mossad and led by an Israeli army officer, dispatched to parts of Europe to track down and kill the members of PLO and Black September responsible for the attack—it was a terrific story, even if the facts were hard to come by and subject to challenge.

Vengeance: The True Story of an Israeli Counter-Terrorist Team, the 1984 account by Canadian journalist George Jonas, was used as a source for *Munich*, as it had been for an earlier television film, *Sword of Gideon*, in 1986. The veracity of Jonas's account was just one of the hot-button issues that would plague the film. The book was based on the recollections of a pseudonymous figure "Avner," whose moral quandaries would become a focal point in both filmed versions.

Had Mossad's emissaries killed the wrong people, underlings rather than the Black September leaders responsible for the attack, as some asserted? Were there civilian casualties, and at least one wrongful death? The Israeli government has never disclosed information on this covert operation; the secret files remain unopened. If *Schindler's List* lit fires of controversy, this would be just as explosive.

The most thorough examination of the facts of the case came from Aaron J. Klein, an Israeli reporter. Perhaps most significant of the inaccuracies Klein alleged was that the unit had no team of Olympic assassins in its sights, just specific targets approved for assassination, including a number of Palestinians who had nothing to do with Munich. According to the reporter, there was no shadowy international organization like "le group," which provides such an alluring European counterweight in the movie. Perhaps most interesting, every one of the fifty-odd veterans of Mossad and Israeli military intelligence whom Klein interviewed was well trained and intent on the mission; none was given to wavering conscience or misgivings after the fact. Spielberg, Klein says, was not alone in buying into the myth; "revenge was in the atmosphere," but the unit's real goal was deterrence.

The effect of the controversy can be gauged by the introduction Spielberg felt compelled to add to the DVD of the film, addressing both the factual issues and the ideological ones. The filmmaker asserts that three facts are indisputable: the attack happened, Golda Meir ordered the reprisal, and the individuals killed were involved in the attack. He asserts his right to fictionalize, stating that his purpose was to explore lessons that emerged and highlight the ongoing dilemma as to how best to fight terrorism. Israel's was the right response, he says, but we are still confronted with difficult, perhaps unanswerable, questions of whether revenge can ever be an efficacious deterrent, rather than simply an eye-for-an-eye expression of visceral need.

Spielberg enlisted as screenwriter Tony Kushner (in collaboration with Eric Roth). This would be the first screenplay by the gifted playwright of *Angels in America*, a bold, even controversial move, as Kushner was an outspokenly left-wing critic of the Israeli government.

To make a film about Israel is almost by definition to get bogged down in argument. Golda Meir's words serve as the film's motto: "Every civilization must negotiate compromise with its own values."

The Middle East was and is and (it seems) ever shall be, at least in our lifetime, a literal and symbolic place of mutually exclusive extremes—no more settlements, an autonomous Palestinian state—with the putative middle ground an ever-receding mirage. But underpinning such seeming intractability is the inescapable fact that the question of Israel's right to exist remains unsettled in the mind of many, and not just in the Arab world.

Munich doesn't go so far as to question Israel's right to retaliate. Yet in both movies made from the Jonas book, we see (as Klein suggests) little of the toughness, the obsessive, even fanatical commitment of both terrorists and counterterrorists; instead, we see the story through the prism of the Western liberal conscience, which by implication stresses the terrible moral toll of revenge.

The ultimate Spielbergian touch, a conversation between Avner (Eric Bana) and a Palestinian, issues in the latter's plea for homeland. Thinking Avner is German, the Palestinian soldier says, "You Europeans, you don't know what it is not to have a homeland. Home means everything." Some will say such scenes smack of "moral equivalence," others that in what we've seen, the moral balance is tilted toward Israel, whose agents are given to spasms of conscience and hand-wringing not experienced by their opponents.

The liberties Spielberg takes, the concessions to Western sensibilities in debating matters of conscience, seem justified, as he tries to illuminate the moral and political shades of gray. Whatever Spielberg's divided loyalties to commercial versus serious filmmaking, he expertly combines the two in a fast-paced, finely tuned balance of action and debate, of zeal and reflection. Part of *Munich*'s appeal is the way it draws on basic genre mythology, the group dynamic of the war film or commando raid, with (in this case) each man representing a different shading of passion for and loyalty to the cause. Your heart is in your throat as Steve (Daniel Craig) and his cohorts roam the world seeking their quarry, in a kind of darkly mordant Jewish variation on the band-of-avengers movie.

Spielberg felt that *Munich* was his most European film, and indeed it does take place in murkier territory than most of his movies, a shadowy world of global connections, unholy alliances, mistrust. Most cheerless of all is what war does to a family, to one's personal life. At one point during the search, while Avner is in Paris and his wife, Daphna, has just had their first baby in Israel, his eye is caught by a fancy display kitchen in a store window. The gleaming appliances radiate the charm of the domestic life that he yearns for and that continually eludes him.

Finally reunited with his wife, however, he finds not peace but constant disturbances from the recent past. In that anomaly for Spielberg, a scene of lovemaking, the director captures what posttraumatic stress might look like. It is awkward and disturbing, something rarely seen on screen. Avner is making love to

Daphna, but his head fills with memories of the massacre and the homicides. It would seem that these images—horrifying and exciting, fight-or-flight triggers—have become embedded in his brain, to the point that they arise reflexively with stimulation of any kind. The passion of lovemaking, of love itself, has been contaminated by the memories of war.

In protecting his homeland, Avner has lost his home.

17

Indiana Jones and the Kingdom of the Crystal Skull, The Adventures of Tintin, *and* War Horse

Indiana Jones and the Kingdom of the Crystal Skull finds sixty-one-year-old Spielberg and sixty-five-year-old Harrison Ford energetically confronting the ultimate enemy, mortality, by acknowledging old age while defying it with every ounce of their being.

The Kingdom of the Crystal Skull takes Harrison Ford's archeologist-adventurer into senior citizenry, his prowess barely diminished. Ford does most of his own stunts—Indy can still kick butt and rescue endangered women—but far from evading the age issue, the movie makes a point of it. With his wizened sex appeal, Indy is a surrogate for aging adolescents of Hollywood, those onetime rebels against the studio fossils, now senior citizens themselves. As the ranks, and the hair, of Hollywood's A-list action stars thin out, a lifeline appears: the geezer superhero movie, with the likes of Sylvester Stallone and Bruce Willis still routing bad guys.

The sense of having to continually prove something contributes to a certain hectic quality in the late films: the need for constant adrenaline shots of wow-wow action, one dazzling pictorial feat after another. After *Crystal Skull*, in which Indy is provided with a sidekick and the franchise with a possible heir (Shia LaBeouf as Indy's newly discovered son), Spielberg tackles animation with a vengeance in 2011's *Tintin*, and then the same year embraces old-fashioned full-blast World War I humanism in the boy-meets-gelding story *War Horse*. (There were fourteen horses of different ages, with their own hair and makeup artist.) Another film, another visual approach. The films are all hits; critical opinion varies. Even when reviewers don't love a film, they marvel at the technical wizardry of something called "pure cinema."

In *Crystal Skull*, we are in 1957, J. Edgar and McCarthy on the march, and Indy's professorial tenure suspended by the FBI. "We've reached the age," mourns his friend the dean (Jim Broadbent), "where life stops giving us things and starts taking them away."

But Indiana Jones was never in the first flush of manhood. I'm discounting the endlessly proliferating television versions meant to cash in on his backstory, a feat of replication that equals the fourteen horses in *War Horse*. He always had a battered, stretched-thin quality and, conveniently for the sex-averse Spielberg, was at first too busy, then too tired for carnal exertions. Witness the scene in the very first installment, *Raiders of the Lost Ark*, when a slinkily dressed Marion comes on to Indy but ends up nursing his wounds as a "love" scene devolves into a snoozefest on Indy's part. "It's the mileage," he groans, closing his eyes.

The franchise ripens into maturity—to the chagrin of some younger fans—in a more personal way, by having Indy come to terms with family at about the same time Spielberg was having his first grandchild. The feeling of settling in extends to the love interest: Marion and Indy's "screwball" exchanges convey more middle-aged pal-ship than electricity, though apparently there is attraction enough to culminate in marriage. A crossover figure, LaBeouf's slacker-dude Mutt seems designed to serve two purposes: for nostalgic geezers, he's a Brando-like rebel; for the young, he's a figure of identification. And a third role: for Indy, he's a dad's worst nightmare.

The ultimate appeal to audiences young and old is presumably the very predictability of the story. For all the technical flourishes and plot twists, the whole series is as formalized as a baroque opera or an Agatha Christie novel. Indeed, there's a certain similarity with the Poirot mysteries, as all the characters, guilty and innocent, gather at the end for the solution of the puzzle. Instead of the vicarage parlor, it's a vast cave, crawling with vipers and scorpions and assorted sexual symbols. Strange noises occur, lights explode, the characters all gape, baffled, like a cowed audience watching an avant-garde play, waiting for meaning to emerge.

And Indy and Marion marry and live happily ever after, or at least until the obstacles presented by the next movie. There is apparently much derring left to do.

Spielberg had been a fan of the great Belgian comic artist Hergé since 1981, and in 2008 he decided to film *Tintin* in a stop motion drama, utilizing the facilities of Peter Jackson's WETA Digital company, the studio that had developed a process of capturing live performance and then digitalizing it into two- or three-dimensional computer animation.

Jackson had used live-action adaptation or motion capture in the *Lord of the Rings* trilogy and *King Kong*, but it was as if the technique had been invented for Spielberg. He was there already. From the beginning, his movies, his characters, the rhythms of plot and movement had been an implicit blend of cartoon and live action, an aesthetic perfectly suited to the presexual boy adventures of which *The Adventures of Tintin* was the latest example. In discussing the absence of any legitimate female character (Bianca the opera singer is more the Shrieking Woman), Manohla Dargis pointed out that Tintin is "as resolutely neutered as his dog presumably is."[1]

Spielberg maintained that as a lover of classical film he always wanted to keep artifice to a minimum. The characters and landscape would have a detailed, photorealist look. Because it was essentially an animated film, he would shoot digitally, while insisting that he would always use film for live action movies.

War Horse was another boy's adventure story, but, as if to prove Spielberg's commitment to the realist spell of film over digital fun-house frenzy, it was also a tribute to old-fashioned filmic storytelling. The sweeping shots of a verdant English countryside (is there any other kind?) might come from a child's coloring book. Though some critics fell in love with the movie, it didn't fare well commercially, and had a glossily packaged feel compared with the virtuosic puppet play adapted by Nick Stafford from Michael Morpurgo's 1982 novel. Spielberg's treatment of nature points up the difference between himself and his idol John Ford, whose landscapes always contained some element of the unpretty and unyielding, a backdrop for characters who were equally stubborn and intractable. Spielberg's nature is Ford seen through Young Adult eyes, green fields and ploughed furrows, all presented in bravura angles and points of view, and begging to be admired.

18

Lincoln *and* Bridge of Spies

The boyish patriarch hangs out on his East Hampton estate, surrounded by wife and brood of seven, hosting barbecues for other parents and children. He's still Steven B. Spielbug, producing and directing at a preposterous rate, while somehow managing to become a family man, as if family has now become his own greatest show on earth.

How did he get from Point A to Point B, from Peter Pan to paterfamilias? His personal journey and "arrival" story is the narrative chronicled in his films. From the celebration of childhood magic to struggles with adult responsibilities, the question arises over and over again: What does it mean to be a boy and then a man in mid-twentieth-century America and beyond? How to grow up in a world in which the values and priorities of masculinity have changed? If his father's World War II generation defined itself, to Spielberg's envy and emulation, by patriotism, stoicism, a fighter spirit, the son has come to appreciate, and to express, a sense of manliness and honor that requires different loyalties.

If his movies sometimes seem old-fashioned, it's because they are concerned with moral responsibility, with what it means to "man up." Families and children remain the bedrock of his vision, but in the post–*Schindler's List* films, the wimp dads of the early films are all but gone. In their place is his own variation on the good father–bad father dichotomy. His allegiance alternates between two types whom he admired or with whom he identified, the flamboyant showman on the one hand, and, on the other, the man of virtue, a family man and ordinary guy who steps up to the plate and achieves a kind of nobility. Such would be the heroes of his next two very different movies, *Lincoln* and *Bridge of Spies.*

The showmen—Steve Ross in real life, Attenborough's Hammond and Neeson's Schindler in the films—had a gift Spielberg also admired and possessed: they could close deals. It must have been a blow, then, when in 2008 he struggled to get financing. In that year, DreamWorks, for the first but not the last time, sought financing overseas. Then the stock market collapsed, and money became even tighter, at which point the negotiations for a partnership with Universal came apart.

The gilt-edged hit maker unable to get backing? News stories feasted on the irony, and the director's mood can't have been improved when Brooks Barnes in the *New York Times* gave voice to a rumor among the cognoscenti that perhaps "the A-list director, at 61, is a little, well, Jurassic?"[1] Eventually a deal was worked out with Disney, but not a favorable one, and for a time he thought he would have to make *Lincoln* for HBO. Such a modest career move, however "freeing" some thought it might be, was less open to Spielberg than ever. *Lincoln* is the very essence of gravitas, a history lesson in epic storytelling mode, and makes its own argument for the scale of Spielberg's ambition down to the mass audience he hopes to reach.

Lincoln, produced with Kathleen Kennedy, was many years in gestation—the longest preproduction since *Schindler's List.* Spielberg, a longtime admirer of Lincoln, had optioned Doris Kearns Goodwin's *Team of Rivals* while she was still at work on it, and engaged Tony Kushner to write the superb screenplay. The masterstroke was constructing the film around the congressional drama of the president's last few months in office, a tumultuous time when he was trying to bring the war to an end, unite a divided country, and abolish slavery. The Emancipation Proclamation had been a temporary measure; he knew how easily it could be dissolved if Congress didn't convert it into a constitutional amendment before the war ended, so this race against time becomes the centerpiece of the film, thereby turning it into a political thriller.

Spielberg brings to life all the tension and contradictions, the backbiting and infighting, the eloquence and farsightedness, the larger-than-life personalities of the shrewd Secretary of State William Seward (David Strathairn) and the fiery abolitionist Thaddeus Stevens (Tommy Lee Jones). The remarkable Daniel Day-Lewis gives Lincoln's struggle weight, immediacy, and interiority, capturing the man's clipped cadences and humor, his personal anguish, his political savvy. We see the cornpone Lincoln, suddenly relaxed when he tells a funny story. We see the private Lincoln, playing with his son but permanently bowed with grief over the deaths of two others, especially the beloved Willie. We see his anguish over his depressed and mentally unstable wife (an extraordinary Sally Field).

The film earned its rave reviews, its place on ten-best lists, its popular esteem and success—a rare congruence of art and commerce. It was nominated for ten Academy Awards, including Best Picture, Best Director, and Best Screenplay. Day-Lewis was awarded Best Actor, but Ang Lee won for directing *Life of Pi.* The award for Best Supporting Actress went to Anne Hathaway in *Les Misérables*, a performance that pales beside Sally Field's brave, wrenching portrayal of the complex and often deeply unlikable Mary Todd Lincoln.

And though it missed the bicentennial, the timing wasn't bad either. The story of the tumultuous end of the president's second term premiered in October 2012 at the New York Film Festival, and in November America reelected its first black president.

David Thomson speculates, not entirely ironically, that Spielberg planned it that way: "He foresaw our moment, he designed his opening, and *Lincoln* is especially momentous as the second Obama administration realizes there is no peace for the elected. It would have had a different resonance if the November 6 result had gone the other way. But Steven—not for the first time—planned an opening that would work either way."[2] In fact, he held back the theatrical release so that it wouldn't open before the election and become campaign fodder for either side.

There were the inevitable charges of inaccuracy, and of hokum. The most egregious example comes when Lincoln, looking both monumental and folksy, engages in a consciousness-raising session with two black soldiers, and then two white soldiers recite the Gettysburg Address. Another blot on the film's escutcheon, and a dark one in a film meant to be used in schools as a history lesson, was an erroneous portrait of the Connecticut representatives, shown as voting for slavery when in fact they voted against.

But even scholars like David Bromwich and Sean Wilentz were inclined to be enthusiastic. Bromwich found tonal lapses alien to Lincoln but considered the drama of the vote and Lincoln's satisfaction at what he had done beautifully expressed.[3] Wilentz, the distinguished Civil War and Reconstruction historian, applauded *Lincoln* as a "monument of American culture" for blowing a hole in the myth of the South as noble loser, that entire tissue of lies perpetrated by the "Lost Cause canon," from Griffith's *Birth of a Nation* through *Gone with the Wind* and beyond.[4]

Unusually for Spielberg, the movie hewed closely to the script, which was an artful symphony of period dialogue and pregnant silences. A formality prevailed on the set: the director dressed in a coat and tie every day and called the actors by their character names. He joked, on a panel after the film's release, that it was especially hard addressing an old friend like Sally Field as Mrs. Lincoln.

A word about that panel, which convened in Richmond, Virginia. Flanked by Goodwin and Kushner, and dressed respectfully in a suit and tie, Spielberg was there to thank the city for providing locations and cooperation in making the film. Now on the stage of a majestic space (once called the Mosque) in the heart of this erstwhile bastion of segregation are: a black man (Tim Reid, the host), a woman, and two Jews, one of them gay. History is being made; the audience is enthralled.

The icing on the cake is a parenthetical remark, one of those glimpses of the off-color so rarely heard from Spielberg—or in Richmond, for that matter. Goodwin, recalling the day she visited the set and marveled at its period details, remembered reading that Erich von Stroheim had his actresses wear silk underwear so that they would feel like wealthy ladies.

"I think it was more to make *Erich* feel something," said Spielberg, with a grin.

Spielberg basked in the afterglow of the film's success. After a screening at the White House, he and the president got into a lively discussion in which Spielberg told Obama about how he uses technology to tell stories. So impressed was Obama that he enlisted Spielberg for a team to help him in the transition from office to life. The director was invited to join a group of celebrity life coaches in concocting something more fun than presiding over the building of a library (*Indy-Obama*, anyone?).

To add to his laurels, Spielberg would be one of three Americans awarded the Presidential Medal of Freedom in November of 2015.

Meanwhile, he had projects lined up for as far as the eye could see: *The BFG*, with Ruby Barnhill, Penelope Wilton, and the great British actor Mark Rylance. A fifth *Indiana Jones*, and *It's What I Do*—Jennifer Lawrence starring in an adaptation of the memoir of Lynsey Addario, the intrepid photojournalist, a woman's film with a vengeance.

Bridge of Spies, Spielberg's 2015 Cold War thriller and Academy Award nominee, is based on the exchange of prisoners following the 1960 U-2 incident. Full of meticulous period details, with dark rain-slick streets, reliably beautiful in the silver, blue-gray tones of Janusz Kaminski's cinematography, the movie, like so many Spielberg period films, reverberates with a sense of present-day anxieties.

There are marvelous shadings among the dubious characters on both sides of the Cold War. In her rave review, Manohla Dargis found it "less weighted down by accreted history or maybe by a sense of duty to its significance" than *Lincoln* or *Munich*.[5] Some of that lightness may be attributable to the Coen brothers' work on the screenplay.

Despite his fascination with planes and aerial exploits, Spielberg is interested not in Gary Powers or in the cunningly designed if ill-fated craft in which he was shot down over Russia, but in the lawyer James Donovan (Tom Hanks) who engineered his release, and the prisoner, Rudolf Abel (Rylance), a British-born Soviet spy, whom he defended and preserved from a death sentence.

Perhaps no one has projected so mysterious a presence in a Spielberg movie, or left so many questions unresolved, as Rylance, the justifiably revered English actor who has become a sort of revisionist villain-hero, making historically unpalatable people captivating. In a thrilling opening he watches himself in the mirror while painting a self-portrait, capturing the multiple identities of the spy's personae. Abel is an evildoer who steals the show like Milton's Satan or one of John le Carré's spies, and his perverse attraction threatens to subvert the moral equilibrium of *Bridge of Spies.* That Abel was here to dig up nuclear secrets for a country that might blow us to smithereens—and that he failed through no fault of his own—is somehow forgotten, or redeemed by his uncompromising patriotism. In the film's climax, we worry about how he will be treated when he returns to the Soviet Union. (For interested readers, *Bridge of Spies: A True Story of the Cold War,* by Giles Whittell, fascinatingly amplifies the backstories of both Abel and Gary Powers.)

The pulsing heart of the movie is the tacit understanding and sense of kinship between lawyer and spy. A fainter heart beats for the family in Brooklyn, the wife (Amy Ryan) and children whom Hanks must leave on his dangerous mission and to which he yearns to return. Donovan, like Lincoln a lawyer, is an ordinary man called upon to face social ostracism and uphold the rights of the hated and disenfranchised. He is also, like Lincoln, deceptive: his folksiness masks the razor-sharp mind of a world-class arguer. Spielberg makes the protagonist (also like Lincoln) more of a regular guy than the real-life model. The actual Donovan was by no means a relative nobody plucked from the lawyer pool but a Fordham- and Harvard-educated attorney of distinction, a cosmopolitan who had argued at the Nuremberg trials. The payoff for Spielberg is, as usual, enhanced audience identification, and Hanks is superb, his Boy Scout virtue balanced by traces of self-mockery.

The theme of manhood has become overt, even self-conscious. Abel honors Donovan with a Russian word that his father used to describe a stand-up guy. The term is reiterated to the point that even the laconic Rylance comes to seem garrulous, and Hanks a dangerous step nearer to canonization.

Donovan has a cold; the man wants to go home. Home

is refuge but also where his responsibilities lie, perhaps in penance for those feckless husbands in the kid-centric films, or for the deserter Roy Neary, who in *Close Encounters* abandoned his family for cosmic adventure. But family reunions never quite fulfill our Christmas-like fantasies, leave expectations hauntingly unmet, and this one is no exception. Too much has happened. The kids are preoccupied with their own lives. Neither they nor his wife can know what he has gone through. A weary Donovan ascends the steps. Like Jamie in *Empire of the Sun* or Elliott in *E.T.*, he is alone with a lingering sense of loss. The deeper bond lies elsewhere, with the alien and soul mate who has returned to the mother ship.

NOTES

1. Beginnings and the Lost Ark

1. Julia Phillips, *You'll Never Eat Lunch in This Town Again* (New York: Random House, 1991).

2. "Spielberg: A Director's Life Reflected in Film," interview by Lesley Stahl, *60 Minutes*, CBS, October 21, 2012.

3. Joseph McBride, *Steven Spielberg: A Biography*, 2nd ed. (Jackson: University of Mississippi Press, 2010), 27.

4. Richard Corliss, "I Dream for a Living," *Time*, July 15, 1985.

5. McBride, *Steven Spielberg*, 16.

2. Steve Bites His Nails and Hears Voices

1. Andy Warhol, prod., "Episode 16," *Andy Warhol's T.V.*, Manhattan Cable TV, New York, July 1982.

2. Joseph McBride, *Steven Spielberg: A Biography*, 2nd ed. (Jackson: University of Mississippi Press, 2010), 40.

3. Richard Corliss, "I Dream for a Living," *Time*, July 15, 1985.

4. McBride, *Steven Spielberg*, 54.

5. Julie Salamon, "Maker of Hit after Hit, Steven Spielberg Is also a Conglomerate," *Wall Street Journal*, February 9, 1987.

6. McBride, *Steven Spielberg*, 55.

7. Neal Gabler, *An Empire of Their Own: How the Jews Invented Hollywood* (New York: Crown, 1988).

3. Arcadia

1. Steven Spielberg, "The Autobiography of Peter Pan," *Time*, July 15, 1985.

2. Joseph McBride, *Steven Spielberg: A Biography*, 2nd ed. (Jackson: University of Mississippi Press, 2010), 70.

3. Ibid., 124.

4. "Spielberg," interview by Ed Bradley, *60 Minutes*, CBS, August 15, 1993.

5. McBride, *Steven Spielberg*, 75.

6. Quoted ibid., 97.

7. There would even be competition in the film world, as Pixar, cofounded by Jobs, would more than hold its own against DreamWorks Animation.

4. The Kid with the Briefcase

1. Joseph McBride, *Steven Spielberg: A Biography*, 2nd ed. (Jackson: University of Mississippi Press, 2010), 111.

2. Bob Hull, "22-Year-Old Tyro Directs Joan Crawford: 'A Pleasure,'" *Hollywood Reporter*, February 17, 1969.

3. McBride, *Steven Spielberg*, 128.

4. Jo Marie Bagala, "Director Wheels Way through Bicycle Epic," *Forty-Niner* (California State College at Long Beach), October 4, 1967.

5. Interviews conducted by McBride with Hill and McNeely.

6. Dilys Powell, *The Sunday Times* (London), October 1972, rpt. in *The Dilys Powell Film Reader*, ed. Christopher Cook (Oxford: Oxford University Press, 1992).

7. Steven Spielberg, "The Autobiography of Peter Pan," *Time*, July 15, 1985.

8. Richard Corliss, "Two from the Heart," *Time*, May 31, 1982.

9. McBride, *Steven Spielberg*, 215, 216.

10. Pauline Kael, "The Sugarland Express," review, *New Yorker*, March 18, 1974.

11. Julia Phillips, *You'll Never Eat Lunch in This Town Again* (New York: Random House, 1991).

5. *Jaws* "Open Wide"

1. Carl Gottlieb, *The Jaws Log* (New York: Newmarket, 2001), 173.

2. Frank Rich, "Easy Living," review of *Jaws*, *New Times*, June 27, 1975.

3. Vincent Canby, "Entrapped by 'Jaws' of Fear," review, *New York Times*, June 21, 1975.

4. Molly Haskell, "The Claptrap of Pearly Whites in the Briny Deep," review of *Jaws*, *Village Voice*, June 23, 1975.

5. Antonia Quirke, *Jaws* (London: British Film Institute, 2002).

6. Robert Phillip Kolker, *A Cinema of Loneliness: Penn, Kubrick, Coppola, Scorsese, Altman* (New York: Oxford University Press, 1980).

7. Arthur Cooper, "The Naked Tooth," review, *Newsweek*, June 23, 1975.

8. Richard Combs, "Primal Scream: An Interview with Steven Spielberg," *Sight and Sound*, Spring 1977.

9. Richard Corliss, "The Seventies: The New Conservatism," *Film Comment*, January 1980, 35.

10. Morris Dickstein, "Peter Panavision," *In These Times*, June 15, 1983.

11. David Puttnam, with Neil Watson, *Movies and Money: Undeclared War between Europe and America* (New York: Knopf, 1998).

12. Tom Shone, *Blockbuster: How Hollywood Learned to Stop Worrying and Love the Summer* (New York: Free Press, 2004).

13. Anthony Breznican, "Steven Spielberg: The EW Interview," *Entertainment Weekly*, December 2, 2011.

6. *Close Encounters of the Third Kind*

1. Susan Sontag, "The Imagination of Disaster," *Commentary*, October, 1965, 42–48.

2. Peter Bart, "David Begelman's Befuddling H'wood Legacy," *Variety*, August 14, 1995.

3. Julia Phillips, *You'll Never Eat Lunch in This Town Again* (New York: Random House, 1991), 139.

4. Paul Schrader and Kevin Jackson, *Schrader on Schrader* (London: Faber and Faber, 1990).

5. Joseph McBride, *Steven Spielberg: A Biography*, 2nd ed. (Jackson: University of Mississippi Press, 2010), 268.

6. Barbara Walters, "1994 Oscar Night Special," *The Barbara Walters Special*, ABC, New York, March 21, 1994.

7. McBride, *Steven Spielberg*, 283.

8. Ibid., 280.

7. *1941* and *Raiders of the Lost Ark*

1. "Show Business: Animal House Goes to War," *Time*, April 16, 1979.

2. Joseph McBride, *Steven Spielberg: A Biography*, 2nd ed. (Jackson: University of Mississippi Press, 2010), 297.

3. Charlton Heston, *In the Arena: An Autobiography* (New York: Simon and Schuster, 1995).

4. Julia Phillips, *You'll Never Eat Lunch in This Town Again* (New York: Random House, 1991), 265.

5. McBride, *Steven Spielberg*, 300.

6. Bob Woodward, *Wired: The Short Life and Fast Times of John Belushi* (New York: Simon and Schuster, 1984), 159.

7. Charles Champlin, "Spielberg's Pearl Harbor," review of *1941*, *Los Angeles Times*, December 14, 1979.

8. McBride, *Steven Spielberg*, 313–14.

9. "Star Wars: The Year's Best Movie," review, *Time*, May 30, 1977.

10. Vincent Canby, review of *Raiders of the Lost Ark*, *New York Times*, June 12, 1981.

8. *E.T.*, *Poltergeist*, and *Twilight Zone*

1. Quoted in Joseph McBride, *Steven Spielberg: A Biography*, 2nd ed. (Jackson: University of Mississippi Press, 2010), 327.

2. John Skow, "Cinema: Staying Five Movies Ahead," *Time*, May 31, 1982.

3. McBride, *Steven Spielberg*, 330.

4. *The Making of "E.T. the Extra-Terrestrial,"* dir. Laurent Bouzereau (1996).

5. Michael Sragow, "A Conversation with Steven Spielberg," *Rolling Stone*, July 22, 1982.

6. Martin Amis, "The World According to Spielberg," *Guardian*, November 21, 1982.

7. Mark Oppenheimer, "Mormons Offer Cautionary Lesson on Sunny Outlook vs. Literary Greatness," *New York Times*, November 8, 2013.

8. Andrew Sarris, "Is There Life after *E.T.?*" *Village Voice*, September 21, 1982, 47.

9. McBride, *Steven Spielberg*, 336.

10. Ibid.

11. Ibid.

12. Ibid., 341.

9. *Indiana Jones and the Temple of Doom* and *The Color Purple*

1. Interview with Dale Pollock, quoted in Joseph McBride, *Steven Spielberg: A Biography*, 2nd ed. (Jackson: University of Mississippi Press, 2010), 350.

2. Vincent Canby, review of *Indiana Jones and the Temple of Doom*, *New York Times*, May 23, 1984.

3. McBride, *Steven Spielberg*, 357.

4. Ibid., 398.

5. Quoted in Jeff Jarvis, "Who's That Woman in the Summer's Smash Movie with What's-His-Name? It's Newcomer Kate Capshaw," *People*, July 2, 1984.

6. McBride, *Steven Spielberg*, 359.

7. Stephen Schiff, "Seriously Spielberg," *New Yorker*, March 21, 1994.

8. Adam Phillips, in "Symposium on Love," *Threepenny Review*, Summer 1993.

9. Molly Haskell, "World of 'The Godfather' No Place for Women," *New York Times*, March 23, 1997.

10. Andrew Borrow, "Filming *The Sugarland Express:* An Interview with Steven Spielberg," *Filmmakers Newsletter*, 1974, 27.

11. Ibid.

12. McBride, *Steven Spielberg*, 363.

13. J. Hoberman, "Color Me Purple," review of *The Color Purple*, *Village Voice*, December 24, 1985.

14. Armond White, review of *The Color Purple*, *Love and Hisses* (1985).

10. *Empire of the Sun*

1. Joseph McBride, *Steven Spielberg: A Biography*, 2nd ed. (Jackson: University of Mississippi Press, 2010), 392.

2. Ibid., 382.

11. *Indiana Jones and the Last Crusade*, *Always*, and *Hook*

1. Quotation: Joseph McBride, *Steven Spielberg: A Biography*, 2nd ed. (Jackson: University of Mississippi Press, 2010), 398.

2. Henry Sheehan, "The Peter Panning of Steven Spielberg," Part 2, *Film Comment*, July–August 1992.

3. McBride, *Steven Spielberg*, 399.

4. Ibid., 411.

12. *Schindler's List*, *Jurassic Park*, and the Shoah Foundation

1. Joseph McBride, *Steven Spielberg: A Biography*, 2nd ed. (Jackson: University of Mississippi Press, 2010), 420.

2. Stephen Jay Gould, "Dinomania," *New York Review of Books*, August 12, 1993.

3. Primo Levi, *The Drowned and the Saved* (New York: Summit, 1988).

4. Stephen Schiff, "Seriously Spielberg," *New Yorker*, March 21, 1994.

5. McBride, *Steven Spielberg*, 442.

6. Ibid., 441.

7. Nicole LaPorte, *The Men Who Would Be King: An Almost Epic Tale of Moguls, Movies, and a Company Called DreamWorks* (Boston: Houghton Mifflin Harcourt, 2010).

8. McBride, *Steven Spielberg*, 445.

9. Schiff, "Seriously Spielberg."

10. Ibid.

13. *Amistad* and *The Lost World: Jurassic Park*

1. "Jurassic World (2015)—International Box Office Results—Box Office Mojo," http://www.boxofficemojo.com/movies/?page=intl&id=jurassicpark4.html, accessed February 21, 2016.

14. *Saving Private Ryan* and *A.I.*

1. "Watershed": Ann Hornaday,"Grace under Fire In 'Saving Private Ryan,' Steven Spielberg Doesn't Flinch from Showing Us War as It Really Is: Bloody, Scary and Loud. And the Stuff of Heroes," review, *Baltimore Sun*, July 24, 1998; "manipulating": Peter Rainer, "Life During Wartime," review of *Saving Private Ryan*, *San Francisco Weekly*, July 22, 1998.

2. Janet Maslin, "Panoramic and Personal Visions of War's Anguish," review of *Saving Private Ryan*, *New York Times*, July 24, 1998.

3. Joseph McBride, *Steven Spielberg: A Biography*, 2nd ed. (Jackson: University of Mississippi Press, 2010), 479.

4. Joe Leydon, "Steven Spielberg and Tom Cruise," *Moving Picture*, June 20, 2002, http://www.movingpictureshow.com/dialogues/mpsSpielbergCruise.html.

5. William Kloman, "In 2001, Will Love Be a Seven-Letter Word?" *New York Times*, April 14, 1968.

15. *Minority Report* and *Catch Me If You Can*

1. J. Hoberman, *Film after Film: Or, What Became of 21st-century Cinema?* (Brooklyn, N.Y.: Verso, 2012).

2. James Naremore, "Love and Death in *A.I. Artificial Intelligence*," *Michigan Quarterly Review* 44, no. 2 (2005).

3. Geoffrey O'Brien, "Prospero on the Run," *Stolen Glimpses, Captive Shadows: Writing on Film, 2002–2012* (n.p.: Counterpoint, 2013), n.p.

16. *The Terminal*, *War of the Worlds*, and *Munich*

1. Matt Wolf, "Hollywood Diary," *Times* [London], 2001 (clipping at Margaret Herrick Library of the Academy of Motion Picture Arts & Sciences).

2. A. O. Scott, "Another Terror Attack, but Not by Humans," review of *War of the Worlds* (2005), *New York Times*, June 29, 2005.

3. "War of the Worlds—Box Office Mojo," last modified February 21, 2016, http://www.boxofficemojo.com/movies/?id=warof theworlds.htm.

17. *Indiana Jones and the Kingdom of the Crystal Skull*, *The Adventures of Tintin*, and *War Horse*

1. Manohla Dargis, "Intrepid Boy on the Trail of Mysteries," review of *The Adventures of Tintin*, *New York Times*, December 20, 2011.

18. *Lincoln* and *Bridge of Spies*

1. Brooks Barnes, "Steven Spielberg's Director's Cut," *New York Times*, July 27, 2008.

2. David Thomson, "Spielberg's *Lincoln* Is a Film for Our Political Moment," review, *New Republic*, November 13, 2012.

3. David Bromwich, "How Close to Lincoln?" *New York Review of Books*, January 10, 2013.

4. Sean Wilentz, "Lincoln in Hollywood, from Griffith to Spielberg," *New Republic*, December 21, 2012.

5. Manohla Dargis, "In 'Bridge of Spies,' Spielberg Considers the Cold War," review, *New York Times*, October 14, 2015.

INDEX

Page numbers in *italics* refer to illustrations.

INDEX

Jewish Lives is a major series of interpretive biography designed to illuminate the imprint of Jewish figures upon literature, religion, philosophy, politics, cultural and economic life, and the arts and sciences. Subjects are paired with authors to elicit lively, deeply informed books that explore the range and depth of Jewish experience from antiquity through the present.

Jewish Lives is a partnership of Yale University Press and the Leon D. Black Foundation.

Ileene Smith is editorial director. Anita Shapira and Steven J. Zipperstein are series editors.

PUBLISHED TITLES INCLUDE:

Ben-Gurion: Father of Modern Israel, by Anita Shapira
Bernard Berenson: A Life in the Picture Trade, by Rachel Cohen
Sarah: The Life of Sarah Bernhardt, by Robert Gottlieb
Leonard Bernstein: An American Musician, by Allen Shawn
Léon Blum: Prime Minister, Socialist, Zionist, by Pierre Birnbaum
Louis D. Brandeis: American Prophet, by Jeffrey Rosen
David: The Divided Heart, by David Wolpe
Moshe Dayan: Israel's Controversial Hero, by Mordechai Bar-On
Disraeli: The Novel Politician, by David Cesarani
Einstein: His Space and Times, by Steven Gimbel
Becoming Freud: The Making of a Psychoanalyst, by Adam Phillips
Emma Goldman: Revolution as a Way of Life, by Vivian Gornick
Hank Greenberg: The Hero Who Didn't Want to Be One, by Mark Kurlansky
Peggy Guggenheim: The Shock of the Modern, by Francine Prose
Lillian Hellman: An Imperious Life, by Dorothy Gallagher
Jabotinsky: A Life, by Hillel Halkin
Jacob: Unexpected Patriarch, by Yair Zakovitch
Franz Kafka: The Poet of Shame and Guilt, by Saul Friedländer
Rav Kook: Mystic in a Time of Revolution, by Yehudah Mirsky
Primo Levi: The Matter of a Life, by Berel Lang

Groucho Marx: The Comedy of Existence, by Lee Siegel
Moses Mendelssohn: Sage of Modernity, by Shmuel Feiner
Moses: A Human Life, by Avivah Zornberg
Proust: The Search, by Benjamin Taylor
Walter Rathenau: Weimar's Fallen Statesman, by Shulamit Volkov
Mark Rothko: Toward the Light in the Chapel, by Annie Cohen-Solal
Solomon: The Lure of Wisdom, by Steven Weitzman
Steven Spielberg: A Life in Films, by Molly Haskell
Barbra Streisand: Redefining Beauty, Femininity, and Power, by Neal Gabler
Leon Trotsky: A Revolutionary's Life, by Joshua Rubenstein